AU REVOIR,
Tristesse

LESSONS *in* HAPPINESS
from FRENCH LITERATURE

VIV GROSKOP

ABRAMS PRESS, NEW YORK

Library of Congress Control Number: 2019939885

ISBN: 978-1-4197-4298-9
eISBN: 978-1-68335-797-1

Printed and bound in the United States
10 9 8 7 6 5 4 3 2 1

Abrams books are available at special discounts when purchased
in quantity for premiums and promotions as well as fundraising or
educational use. Special editions can also be created to specification.
For details, contact specialsales@abramsbooks.com or the
address below.

Abrams Press® is a registered trademark of Harry N. Abrams, Inc.

ABRAMS The Art of Books
195 Broadway, New York, NY 10007
abramsbooks.com

AU REVOIR,
Tristesse

ALSO BY THE AUTHOR

The Anna Karenina Fix: Life Lessons from Russian Literature

CONTENTS

INTRODUCTION

Happiness is . . . pretending to be French

"Savoir, penser, rêver. Tout est là."
("To know, to think, to dream. It's all there is.")

—VICTOR HUGO

THERE IS ONE VERY OBVIOUS life lesson the French want to teach us: If you want to be happy, it's best to be French. If you want to lead the ideal kind of life, then that life is to be found in France. Françoise Sagan is the embodiment of this. She is a joyously indifferent shrug in human form. She embodies joie de vivre and the freedom to do whatever the hell you want. That, surely, is what most of us define as happiness? Taking real pleasure in every moment, eating the best food, drinking the best drink, falling in love, following your passions . . . The French think they do all this better than the rest of us. And Françoise Sagan looks as if she does it even better than the average French person. She may have written a novel entitled *Bonjour Tristesse (Hello Sadness)*. But she embodies the idea of Au Revoir, Tristesse (Goodbye, Sadness). And isn't sadness the one thing we all want to say goodbye to?

I first encountered Sagan on British television in the 1980s. I was watching a BBC travel documentary, *Postcard from Paris*, hosted by the Australian broadcaster Clive James, which was a phenomenon in Britain at the time. This television show was so popular, Clive James wrote later in the *New Yorker*, that even Princess Diana videotaped it if she was

1

going out. In the show, James wandered around by the banks of the Seine looking dreamy and wistful, interviewed French celebrities—although no men were interviewed in this program, only attractive women—and in one episode, he was chauffeured by Françoise Sagan in her own car. Sagan pulls up in a screech of tires, apparently wearing no seat belt, and off they go at around ninety miles per hour through a built-up area. "It is quite quick, this car," says James nervously in slow English so that she can understand. Later, he adds: "You really like speed, don't you?" She doesn't take the hint.

"Life is so slow," says Sagan lazily. As she is driving him around Paris as if her white Citroën were an emergency vehicle, he attempts to interview her while she attempts to break the speed limit. She shrugs nonchalantly about the serious car crash she had at the age of twenty-one, from which she emerged with almost every bone in her body broken: "Eleven ribs, two wrists, and the head open. They thought I was dead. They closed my eyes." As she's telling this gruesome accident story, she hits a pedestrian and drives on, still shrugging, as James whimpers quietly. A voiceover breaks in: "We only hit his briefcase. But the impact left him spinning in the street like a weathervane."

This footage played in my mind's eye quite a while, and I would often remember it and chuckle to myself. Goodbye, sadness, indeed. But when I came to look for this documentary, years later, I couldn't find it. Unlike Princess Diana, I hadn't been smart enough to record it. I began to wonder if I had invented it. After all, it was my own personal fantasy of what it meant to be a certain kind of French person. You drove around Paris not minding what anyone thought of you, hitting pedestrians' briefcases and not giving a damn. By this point I could speak quite a bit of the language and was hoping the effects of that were turning me French. Maybe without the homicidal bit. Sagan's behavior was the dream. A slightly monomaniacal and evil dream, yes. But the dream. Or at least a watered-down version of it. Even if it felt a bit too outlandish to be true. Was it so much of a dream that it was in fact an actual dream?

Then, suddenly, a couple of years ago, when I was Googling something else, I stumbled across the video and I was transported back to that moment. Turns out it was from 1989. It was the voiceover that really hit me in a jolt of recognition; Clive James's slow, deliberate, cynical Australian drawl. In the introduction he is describing a phenomenon that can only be experienced by reading a writer that you love. He quotes Sagan: "Something wells up in me that I greet by name: 'Bonjour, tristesse.'" He continues, as the camera pans across the Pont des Arts: "Françoise Sagan was seventeen years old when she wrote that, and she was here, a writer in Paris. I was at the other end of the world, dreaming about being a writer in Paris. I dreamed of Left Bank café tables, where I would sit writing my own sensationally precocious novel, called *Au Revoir, Sydney*." Here was the proof I had experienced when I first saw that film: This is a way that people feel. Other people feel this way. It is real.

The desire to escape ourselves and find a better way to live is a huge part of the reading experience. The novelist Jeanette Winterson calls reading "a lifelong collision with minds not like your own." Learning a language and discovering the writers who wrote in that language is a double collision. You access the mind-set of another culture through language. And you access it deeper through reading. This was the hard-core collision I wanted, and it was the hotline to the particular kind of French happiness I craved. I had spent my teen years dreaming of the exact same thing as Clive James: Au revoir, boring England! Bonjour, Paris! It was a love affair that started with school French lessons at the age of eleven and was reinforced by summers spent in France during my adolescence. By the time I was old enough to discover the great French writers not just on TV but properly, I was completely hooked.

That television footage was the start of an obsession with these authors, beginning with Sagan, who was one of the easiest and most attractive places to start, especially for a teenager. I wanted to read their stories in order to understand their world, to understand them, to think like them. To be less myself and more, well, French. Sagan's attitude in that interview represented something extraordinary for me. Here was a woman who lived life in a reckless, impetuous, and selfish way. She was unlike anyone I had ever seen before. She was free. Almost too free. Free enough to knock people over in the street and not care about it. I wasn't sure exactly what this was supposed to teach me about how to live a better life. But I felt that if I tried hard enough, it would seep into me. Although I had a few reservations. Surely if you want to live a good life, you should try not to run people over? I decided not to think too much about this. I could sense there was something elusive, intriguing, and important about the French way of thinking about life and about happiness. They followed slightly different rules than the rest of us. And maybe if I could learn those rules, I could live like them.

I suppose this was less about wanting to be more French and more about wanting to be less like myself. I was at an age when I was looking for a way of being and I was trying to decipher the signs the adult world was offering me. The documentary was not only about what Sagan was like; it was about what a different kind of person she was compared to the interviewer. Clive James is a supremely intelligent and admirable man. His whole career as a broadcaster was based on analyzing culture, enjoying literature, and appreciating the finer things in life. And as he breathes the air in Paris in that clip, you can tell that he has met his match: this place is better even than him. He represented what everyone who isn't French and wants to be French thinks about the French. To be in Paris with Sagan brings him joy. But it also tortures him. He wants to speak French, he wants to be French, and most of all, he admits, he wants to be with a French woman. But he cannot do or be any of these things, and he is "consumed with the sadness of the unattainable." Watching this, at sixteen, and with several years of French lessons under my belt, I sighed and made a lifelong vow: to hell with the sadness of the unattainable. There must be another way. Let the French writers show it to me.

These pages, then, are an exploration of a feeling: the elusive something I was looking for when I saw this woman on my TV screen, driving like a maniac, waving her cigarette out the window and pouting angrily underneath a too-long fringe of artfully messed-up hair. (It was probably this fringe that prevented her from seeing the man with the briefcase. That, and her general indifference toward pedestrian safety.) The French have invented all the words for this feeling. *Un certain je-ne-sais-quoi.* The indefinable certain something. *La joie de vivre.* The joy of being alive. *Le bien-être*, which sounds so much sexier and more exciting than the mealy-mouthed, goody-goody, Goop-esque "well-being." It is this spirit of grabbing life by the throat and not caring about what others think. Is this true happiness, then, this Frenchness? The freedom to do what you want? That sense of abandon? What is it about this attitude to life that is appealing and particularly French? It feels like a combination of two middle fingers up to authority, knowing what you want, mastering yourself, and getting somewhere you want to be in a hurry. Riding life instead of letting life ride you. That is the French version of the meaning of life that we are drawn to. Even their word for happiness makes you smile: *le bonheur.* Literally "the good hour." That's all we're really looking for, isn't it? One good hour at a time.

When I was growing up in a small town in rural England in a solidly English environment, this mentality appealed greatly to me. I certainly could not see it reflected anywhere around me. Over the years of my adolescence I accumulated pieces of evidence that people lived differently in France. This gave me great inspiration and hope for the future. There were other places where people did whatever the hell they wanted and not only did others let them do it, they applauded them for it! They ate frogs' legs and snails. They drank hot chocolate out of gigantic bowls at breakfast. They dipped their bread into their drinks. This kind of Continental behavior was not the case in my childhood or in rural England. And, yes, this was a time when people in the UK still referred to France and the rest of Europe as "the Continent." If something was racy or fun or not properly British, it was "a bit Continental." I began to see life in England through the eyes of the French. Our vegetables were overcooked and mushy. Like baby food. Or like something you would feed to someone who had lost their teeth. We put so much milk in our tea that it was virtually milk. We bought bread that was so full of artificial substances that you didn't have to eat it on the same day. You could eat it three days later. The French are particularly suspicious of this kind of bread-eating. I began to think of my own people as barbarians.

And it was a form of barbarism that was a prison. At home in England I was expected to conform and be a certain kind of person: not too ebullient, not too loud, not too passionate, discreetly cynical about everything. Frenchness offered an escape and represented something so exciting for me: dynamism, energy, heat, the equivalent of driving a clapped-out Citroën at ninety miles per hour through central Paris. Certainly there was a feminist element for me here too. Not only were people in general discouraged from behaving in this reckless way in the environment in which I grew up, but women in particular would be seen as odd if they behaved like Sagan. Her version of living was radical, rebellious, and exciting.

On my first proper visit to France as an adolescent, I tried to use my schoolgirl French to blend in. I began to pick up things that I had not been taught in school by using a method I now think of as "situational." Situational learning is how most people learn a language. You use what you've got, and you muddle through. You don't hold back from speaking just because you don't have the perfect words. You observe situations and copy what native speakers say in those situations. When I was twelve, I went on my first school exchange to Angers in the Loire Valley and lived with a French family for two weeks. My French was minimal, and I could only describe what had happened in the past by adding the word "yesterday" to very short sentences—"Yesterday, I go to the cinema," "Yesterday, I eat *pain au chocolat*"—but I was determined to blend in even if it meant speaking like an idiot. Partly it was about escapism and novelty. I see that. But also it was about being able to communicate and connect in an unexpected way. And if you were willing to make a fool of yourself (and I was), you could make people laugh. "Yesterday, I go to the cinema. Yesterday, I like the film. Today, I do not like the film. *C'est la vie.*" Yes, I was a twelve-year-old female Frasier Crane. I often felt frustrated at how slow I was to make progress in French, and I wondered how many years it would take me to be fluent (answer: about seven or eight). But I also felt a sense of possibility and excitement.

This for me was the main point of French: finding ways to remember how to say things in another language that had nothing to do with learning by rote and everything to do with silliness and fun. French accessed a crazy, literal, eccentric part of my brain. I loved reminding myself that in French you had to say, "I wash myself the hands" (*"Je me lave les mains"*) instead of just "I wash my hands." These things tickled me for some reason, and some warped part of me enjoyed learning two things at once: (a) a pointless and weird way of saying something in English that no one would ever say ("Until the re-seeing!") and (b) the actual way of saying it in French (*"Au revoir!"*). I find it almost impossible to believe that you are not changed as a person if, instead of saying something as prosaic and dull as "I need to wash," you say things like "It is necessary that I wash myself the hands" (*"Il faut que je me lave les mains"*).

The diligent acquisition of the French language domi-nated my teenage years, and I wanted to speed up the process as much as possible. I visited my pen pal's family twice a year, and she visited me in England once a year. It was a very unfair "exchange," as she just gave up on learning English after a while as I was incredibly pushy and would only talk to her in French. If this reflects badly on me, please know that she did not make much effort to push back. In between these visits I would watch a subtitled French soap opera called *Châteauvallon*, which was screened on British television and was mostly about married people having sex with people they were not supposed to have sex with. Having heard the gabbled stream-of-consciousness that is French radio, I knew the practice we got at school was not going to get me very far. I would try to tune into French radio on my own radio set, specially procured for this reason, and when I could get a clear enough signal, I recorded French live radio on cassettes and then played it back for my own DIY listening practice. Meanwhile, to improve my written French, I had an ever-increasing number of French-speaking pen pals in addition to the French friend I already visited: from Laurence in Belgium, who sent me pictures of pop star Jean-Jacques Goldman cut out of magazines, to Patou, a French Vietnamese girl from Normandy who sent me pictures of her cat. Basically, I was a sort of one-woman living Wikipedia of Frenchness, snorting up every little croissant crumb of culture and language I could find.

I feel so sorry for my parents when I think about what I put them through, having to live with me as I attempted to survive in a small English town in the middle of nowhere with no internet and intermittent access to foreign-language magazines. I was gripped by a sort of frenzy. This was not so much Francophilia as Francomania. I had posters on my wall of Johnny Hallyday ("the French Elvis") and Sandra Kim (the 1986 Eurovision entry for Belgium whose hairstyle was, I thought, a chic twist on Princess Diana's and upon whom I modeled my style for three years). I was fascinated by the strange lyrics of

French pop songs, which I attempted to decipher and translate, never quite sure whether my translation was completely wrong or the French were just incredibly weird. I became obsessed with a Johnny Hallyday lyric from the song *"Que Je T'Aime"* ("How I Love You"): *"Mon corps sur ton corps / Lourd comme un cheval mort."* "My body on your body / Heavy like a dead horse." Why would anyone say this? Or even think it? Why? What was I missing about the erotic experience of having a dead horse on top of me? Why was Johnny Hallyday boasting about being as heavy as a dead horse? Such were the mysteries I wished to unravel, hopefully without having to kill a horse and lie naked under it. It was only a matter of time before I started trying to read Proust and learn Baudelaire poems by heart.

This, then, is a book about the intersection between Frenchness and happiness through reading, as that is a place I have always found great comfort. My hope is to demonstrate, through the French writers I first discovered in my teens and twenties, how that intersection might help us all get more joy into our lives. The novelist André Gide once described joy as a moral obligation: "Know that joy is rare, more difficult, and more beautiful than sadness. Once you make this all-important discovery, you must embrace joy." Was it an accident in some ways, that French brought so much joy into my life? Could it have been any language, any hobby, any discovery? Or was it something intrinsic about the Frenchness that created the joy? Later on, I studied German and Spanish at school, and much later on I became completely obsessed with Russian, which became a whole other story. But French was my first love, and I managed to learn it well enough that I still speak it fluently now, over thirty years after my first lesson and without much regular practice. French has been a constant in my life. It is a part of me. Being able to dip into the books mentioned in these pages in order to keep that part of me alive has been a wonderful thing to cling to through life's ups and downs.

The French being the French, I suspect they would claim that it is very much not an accident that their literature is meaningful and life-changing. After all, they have laid claim to many important things in life, far greater even than wine, cheese, or sex. (And truly they have laid claim—definitively—to all these things as if they, and only they, invented them.) Over the years, the French have asserted that they have the most beautiful and most expressive language, the utmost clarity of thought in the history of human thinking, and, of course, the greatest propensity for experiencing joy. They have laid all this out in extensive detail through the words of Voltaire, Rousseau, Descartes, and Montaigne. But it can all be encapsulated very quickly and easily in a few words. French equals best.

I wonder if it was this confidence—arrogance, even, let's be honest here—that first attracted me to the French language, and, by extension, French literature. There's a swagger to French thinking that is not shared by other cultures. If you are looking for joy, wonder, happiness, life, and light, then you are more likely to look for those elusive things in a place that really looks like it knows what it's doing, a place where the people are not afraid to tell everyone else that they know exactly what they're doing and are very happy doing it. The French have never been shy to say this. Of course there is great life-affirming joy and élan in the life of many, many other cultures. But come on. When the French even own the words for expressing those things, you've got to admit that they've beaten the rest of us before we've even started.

A Note on the Reading List

Why have I chosen the works I have chosen in this book? And why is there no Rousseau, Voltaire, Baudelaire, Nerval, Apollinaire, [insert the name of your favorite writer here]? I have no good answer to these questions. The truth is that these are the writers and the works I am personally most interested in, know most intimately, and wanted to revisit. Some of them I discovered by accident. Some were introduced to me, such as Maupassant, who was read to us in class by my school French teacher, Mr. Harley. Others were simply the most prominent titles on my compulsory university reading list. Others I found later in life. The list here makes up what I would say is a very basic and obvious introduction to French literature. It's not an attempt at any kind of alternative reading list, and it is probably fairly old-fashioned and predictable. I'm influenced by the books I loved when I first discovered them—around the age of eighteen or nineteen mostly—and less by the books I found out about later, which were arguably cooler and more interesting. Of course, I'm afraid that there are not many women because this is a book trying to look at the appeal of the books that have long been considered the classics. And I cannot rewrite history and how the classics became the classics. (See A Note on Other Writers, page 243, for the necessary disclaimer about women writers, and more generally, writers who are not white, male, middle-aged, and middle-class, and for further reading recommendations.)

These are—crucially—all books that deserve to be preserved as important landmarks in global culture. The order they appear in this book is not unintentional: I have ranked them according to which is most likely to lead to happiness, in order of the most cheery (which, er, ends in what is probably a suicide) to the least joyful (which ends in an execution). I found in making my selection of classics that offer a lesson in happiness that my "happy" feelings around a book did not necessarily have to do with what happened in the book. Many of the things that happen in these books are extremely unfortunate, from multiple instances of adultery resulting in murder (*Le Rouge et Le Noir*) and death on the battlefield (*Cyrano de Bergerac*) to being dumped by the person you love the most in the world (*L'Amant*) and botched club foot operations (*Madame Bovary*). Don't worry, these are not things that make me happy. Here's where the joy is: in the writing, in how the Frenchness is revealed, and in what they have to teach us about life. I also found as I was revisiting a lot of these authors that although there were details of their worlds that were life-affirming (suppers featuring exclusively onion dishes, Campari cocktails, moustaches so lavish that they were virtually animate), in the main they were depressed, promiscuous, alcoholic, overworked, grumpy, and, in a great many cases, suffering from syphilis. I set out to write a love letter to my favorite authors, and I ended up with a book by my bedside entitled *Pox: Genius, Madness and the Mysteries of Syphilis*. It turned out that in some cases (Maupassant, I am looking at you), an encyclopedia of sexually transmitted diseases was more key to understanding French literature than a dictionary. It's all very well to attempt to master the art of happiness. It's also important to recognize that it might sometimes come at a price.

This book also represents a sort of a corrective. I get a bit stressed sometimes, thinking about whether anyone is really bothering with these books anymore. For me as a teenager they represented glamour, luxury, excitement, exoticism, adulthood, and secret knowledge. I'd like to think they can still hold their own against the latest digital innovations competing for our time. But I know from my university tutors that the eighteen-year-olds of today simply read a lot fewer novels than we did. I mention this without judgment, as had the internet been invented twenty years earlier, I'm not sure I would ever have picked up a book. But that is what makes these books even more important. On social media we suck up every piece of advice going, from the best way to start your day to the amount of sleep we need. We tolerate our screens being clogged with "life hacks" from social media influencers. Again, I say this without judgment, as I devour all these things too and frequently enjoy them enormously. But what's shocking—and refreshing—about returning to the French classics is that they already contain all the wisdom that we need about the pitfalls and pleasures of the ideal life. And they have been sitting on the bookshelves waiting there for us all along. Reading these books at your leisure on a chaise longue (real or imaginary) is a whole lot more fun than Googling "Why do I feel so depressed?" at three in the morning. And arguably they will produce a more tangible and longer-lasting effect on your well-being than an internet search. I know because I've tried both.

That said, these books are not holy, mystical texts that hold the key to life. Often they're flawed. Or the passage of time has not been kind to them. Sometimes both. I have been thinking a lot recently about what constitutes a classic and whether our definition of this needs to change in the twenty-first century. Or if it will change, whether we like it or not. Clearly we can't rewrite what have already been classed as "classics." But I do think our evaluation of these things is shifting in the current era, not least because there is so much competition for our time and attention now that the published word occupies a very different place in the cultural hierarchy compared to one hundred or one hundred fifty years ago.

We often approach books—and especially fiction—that contain big, important ideas differently now, sadly. These books are sometimes seen more as an obligation and less as an important statement about our times. A lot of this has to do with the changing views toward "gatekeepers" (publishers, editors, taste makers of all kinds) who have accompanied the advent of the internet. And some of it is to do with what we regard as significant. The role, for example, that people like Jean-Paul Sartre, Simone de Beauvoir, Françoise Sagan, or Marcel Proust occupied at the heart of Western culture while they were alive was very specific. I'm not sure that the sorts of people who occupy those roles now are treated the same way, nor do their works necessarily sell in the same numbers. I sometimes wonder whether some of these people, if they existed now, would just be on Twitter all the time and would not insist on writing dozens of books. Balzac, for example, the original keyboard warrior, could microblog the ninety-one-novel series that is *La Comédie Humaine* in real time.

This book concentrates on twelve classics of French literature that best represent my own reading taste. In the same way that we all love the things we know the best, they seem like obvious choices. But I'm well aware that it might make people cry big hot Sauternes-hued tears to see that Alexandre

Dumas's *Musketeers*, Baudelaire's *Les Fleurs du Mal*, and Molière's farces are not here. I could have included other authors I studied at university—Jean-Paul Sartre, Louis-Ferdinand Céline, Simone de Beauvoir, or the playwrights Jean Anouilh and Eugène Ionesco—although those last two would have given me terrible flashbacks. I acted with great, earnest enthusiasm in French language amateur dramatic versions of *L'Alouette* and *Le Roi Se Meurt* at university—both male roles, I seem to recall, very possibly with a drawn-on moustache. But I think the list represents a comprehensive and realistic canon of French literature that is not unlike my own university reading list but is still accessible to anyone who isn't naturally drawn to the idea of reading 1.25 million words of Proust, the actual word count of *À La Recherche du Temps Perdu*.

All the books here have sold internationally in millions of copies and—more significantly for the case at hand—have something deep and significant to say about French culture. I wanted to cover books that have reached a huge readership: books where copies shifted en masse. Of course, there's no way to cover every single angle and every single important development. And I have some regrets about not having included one particular book that achieved a singular success in Paris in the twentieth century. As Agnès Poirier writes in *Left Bank: Art, Passion and the Rebirth of Paris 1940–1950*, the sales of Jean-Paul Sartre's *L'Être et Le Néant (Being and Nothingness)* benefited from a big boost in sales figures in 1947. Sartre found out that women were buying the book because it weighed exactly one kilogram. It was a particularly useful household item at a time when copper weights had been melted down for munitions. (Stick that in your existentialist subconscious, philosopher!)

All the editions I have used here are mentioned in the Recommended Reading list at the end of the book. I haven't chosen special, favorite translations; I have chosen whatever was to hand. And mostly I have used translations because I find that they are quicker to read and reference than reading in the original. I have experienced every extreme of reading in French: from plowing through Marcel Pagnol using a dictionary for every fifth word through to reading Proust in the original. I don't spend as much time in France as I would like, but I find that as long as I pick up a book in French from time to time, I'm still comfortable reading it. It's not easy to read literature in the language it was written in if it's not your first language. But I reached a point in French where I could manage it, usually most easily at the times in my life when I was living in France and thinking and dreaming in French. Now, it's something meditative and enjoyable, especially if I can read something that is short and easy and can make me feel smug because it hasn't been translated into English yet.

On the other hand, I am a great defender of reading in translation. To translate a text is a great skill in its own right, and many translations have their own special beauty, separate to the original. The question always comes up, though, especially for people who don't know the language: Can we ever be sure that we are understanding everything when we are reading in translation? I understand this fear. You don't want to feel as if you're going to the trouble of reading something only to realize that you're reading it all wrong. And, to be fair, there are many concepts, ideas, and words that don't have a precise match between French and English. Already one of the awkwardnesses of translation emerged with the title of this book. I wanted to conjure up something that expressed the joy, playfulness, and delightful Frenchness of *Bonjour Tristesse* while evoking the idea that this was a book that wanted to be rid of sadness, welcoming in joy instead. The opposite translation seemed to me to be *Au Revoir, Tristesse*. I didn't even think that it could be anything else.

Then I came to reread *Bonjour Tristesse* for the first time in thirty years and realized that the novel is inspired by the first line of a poem by Paul Éluard that begins "Adieu Tristesse." That's also an accurate translation. Which is better? Immediately I was thrown into the confusion of my pedantic eleven-year-old self, discovering French for the first time and feeling infuriated that it was impossible to know when you should say "adieu" and when you should say "au revoir" and feeling that it was incredibly important to know the difference. For some reason, no one explained to me: "Adieu means 'farewell.' And when was the last time you said 'farewell' to someone?" So instead, as a young French learner, I was left wondering why I was so stupid that I didn't even know the difference between these two very different types of goodbye.

For a long time I pondered this and even sometimes wanted to take it literally and say to French boys who had made it obvious that they didn't want to be my boyfriend "Adieu" (literally "To God"—or, as far as I was concerned, "I hope you go to God, i.e., that you die"). To French boys who had been kind to me—or who had, at least, not humiliated me, I said, "Au revoir," or "Until the re-seeing!" These are the little nuances that we worry that we are missing out on when we read translations. But we really need to let go of these things because, seriously, when someone says "au revoir" to you in

French, then they are not literally thinking, "I am already planning to re-see this person." Although I would worry if someone said "adieu" to me. Just saying. They might know something I don't.

As a side note, it is worth saying that there are some things that I think you can only get away with saying in French that do lose something in translation. The Paul Éluard poem that serves as an epigram for the novel *Bonjour Tristesse* is from his collection *La Vie Immédiate*. This in itself is a cheering title for a collection (*Immediate Life*, or, perhaps, *Life in Close Proximity*), and nothing as depressing as the title of the poem that contains the line "Bonjour Tristesse," the title of which is *"À Peine Défigurée"* ("Barely Disfigured"). It's a seemingly depressing, enigmatic, and extremely French poem, which appears to refer to someone you would not want to re-see particularly soon.

I was shocked when I discovered that the title of *Bonjour Tristesse*—a joyful, profound novel—was taken from this strange, slight poem. The title of the poem particularly annoyed me. The idea of being "barely disfigured" seemed cruel and unambiguous to me. In translation it came across very harsh. But then I tried to take in the poem in French, and I felt completely differently about the whole thing. It's a poem not about a person but about sadness. It imagines sadness as a person, lightly disfigured. This fits in perfectly with the ideas and themes of Françoise Sagan's novel. Éluard writes, addressing sadness as if it were a person: "You cannot be pure misery / As the poorest lips can denounce you / With a smile." This is a basic idea, but it's a delightful one that reveals the true meaning of many of the books here. No matter how much sadness there is, it can always be punctured by an unexpected human connection. Sadness is everywhere. But it can be countered at any time.

Some Rules of Engagement

Do you need to know French in order to read this book? *Absolument pas.* (No, you don't.) I was recently reminded that even extremely intelligent people who I hold in excessively high regard do not necessarily speak French. I tend to assume that such people do speak French, purely as my own form of confirmation bias. *Cogito ergo sum.* I like you, therefore you must speak French. I was slightly horrified when I went to see Michelle Obama speak in Paris as part of her European book tour that she very obviously doesn't speak any French. I admire her so much that I just assumed that she would. Not only did she not even say *"bonsoir"* (good evening) or *"merci"* (thank you) to the crowd of forty thousand who had gathered to see her (and who had the backup of a simultaneous interpreting app they could listen to on headphones), but she also referred to eating *"crêpes fromage,"* which made me almost weep with disappointment. There is no such thing as *"crêpes fromage."* It's like saying that you had a pancake with cheese. I feel on pretty solid ground in thinking that no British or American person would ever order a pancake with cheese. I got quite angry about this, thinking that Michelle Obama had been heinously missold a crêpe.

This taught me an important lesson: me liking someone doesn't make them fluent in French. It's simply a fact that many people don't know the languages they would like to know. Maybe they never had the opportunity to learn. Or maybe they had a teacher who didn't engage them. I'm one of the lucky ones: French was compulsory at my school from the age of eleven. And I had great French teachers who infused me with a love of the language and the country. Even without the language, though, you can get so much from the literature in translation. You don't need to know a word of French to read this book, nor to appreciate French authors more generally. Much as I have devoted my life to the study of language and much as speaking foreign languages has been one of the greatest joys of my existence, I do not judge others who don't want to do this, who don't have the chance or even who think that speaking foreign languages is for losers.

I experienced this in my own family. While my grandmother was open-minded and saw learning languages as a means of social mobility and changing your life (and this became true for me), my grandfather was a diehard patriot who believed that allowing foreign words to invade your mouth was tantamount to treason and may cause you physical harm. The most we could ever get him to say in French was "inky-pinky parlez vous" and "comma pally tally vous." To be fair, he enjoyed saying these things greatly and wheeled them out as his party trick.

As my grandad was well-aware, the trouble with speaking a foreign language is that it can be a sign of pretension. It's often used to intimidate people, to try to appear cleverer than you really are. Or to try to trick people. I'm reminded again of my favorite French speaker, Frasier, and the scene where Niles and Frasier tiptoe around Eddie talking in French so that the dog won't know that he is going to the vet. (*"Tu es celui qui va l'amener chez le médecin pour le snip-snip."* "You are the one who is going to take him to the doctor for the snip-snip.") There's even a scene in *Friends* where Joey Tribbiani says something in "French" that is very similar to my grandad's pretend franglais. Phoebe—a fluent French speaker played by the superb Lisa Kudrow—is coaching Joey for an audition where he has to read some lines in French. He believes he is speaking French, but in fact he is talking gibberish. Or what might be described as fake drunk French: "Flou balou de laclou bombadou." In the end she has to persuade the director to humor Joey and let him down gently when he tells him he hasn't got the role. Joey is thrilled and expresses his joy in fluent French: "Blabada!" Put simply: whether your French is fluent, inky-pinky, or blabada, you are safe here. Nothing here is meant to intimidate, confuse, or bamboozle you into thinking that you're going on a nice trip when in fact you are going for a surgical procedure to remove your testicles. Eddie, Joey, and my grandfather would be welcome to read this book.

Will this book help you learn French? No. But I very much hope it will make it seem like a good idea. All the same, I'm very keen for readers to know that I am not going to be indulging in the temptation to "*parler français*" at every available moment in this book. As I think that would be insufferable. By which I mean that I will only use French words where I think it's strictly necessary and I won't be throwing into the narrative just to add a little bit of épice (spice). See how annoying it would become? The only exception is that I'm using the original French titles of the books because I want to. And because they sound beautiful. My justification is that we all need what my (small-amount-of-French-speaking) grandma would call "a little bit of ooh-la-la" in our lives. And also that these books are so well-known by their original names that it seems a shame to saddle them with the clumsy, heavy English equivalents that their authors very much did not mean to write. *À La Recherche du Temps Perdu*? Ah, just listen to what that evokes. *In Search of Lost Time*? It sounds like a *Star Trek* episode.

In real life, I am a constant practitioner of exactly the kind of random French insertion that I will be avoiding within these pages. I know it's horrific, but I am happy to own it. If some poor, innocent French person is chatting away, I will usually go up to them and say (in French), "Excuse me, are you French?" Which is a stupid question because they clearly are. And I will then attempt to engage them in conversation. My children and husband are extremely practiced at looking at the ground and pretending not to be present. This is a habit I picked up from a young age, encouraged by my grandmother, growing up in the countryside in England, where I hardly ever met anyone and feared that I would never really be able to speak a foreign language because I just was not getting enough practice. The main keys to learning a language? Immersion, making thousands of mistakes, and engaging people in conversation even if you can tell that they don't really want to talk to you and wish you would go away. This last bit is particularly true of French people when speaking to a British person. I usually pretend that I have a French parent. It's a lie, but it helps.

So while I believe that using French, especially when French people are around, is incredibly important, I hate exclusivity. Slipping into French to make yourself appear intelligent is the adult equivalent of what aristocratic parents used to say when conversation turned controversial: *"Pas devant les enfants"* ("Not in front of the children"). I don't want to patronize or irritate readers who are not French speakers. And I don't want to put anyone off from learning even a small amount of French by bombarding them with Proustian flights of fancy in the original. A little bit of French is acceptable. But only *un petit peu*. (OK, I will stop now.)

Attention aux spoilers! (Translation: Beware spoilers!)

Yes, I know I said I wasn't going to use too much French, but I couldn't resist that one. Apparently the word "spoiler" is used as much in French as it is in English. So that is refreshing. If you know the word "spoiler" and can say it in an "ooh-la-la" way, then you already speak French. Well done! So what about spoilers for all these books that have been around for up to three hundred years? As the novelist Rachel Cusk writes in her 2008 introduction to the Penguin Modern Classics edition of *Bonjour Tristesse*: "New readers are warned that the introduction reveals details of the plot." And why shouldn't it, when *Bonjour Tristesse* was published fifty-four years before? In relation to this edition, that just about says it all. Readers of all kinds are warned that this book reveals details of absolutely everything. So if there are particular novels that you have been wanting to read your whole life and you want to discover them without knowing anything about them in advance . . . Well, this would be the moment to look away from that particular chapter. As the young people say: Sorry not sorry.

This type of spoiler acceptance is familiar territory for me. I wrote a book about the classics of Russia entitled *The Anna Karenina Fix: Life Lessons from Russian Literature*, and despite ample warnings and disclaimers in the text about spoilers and how they were simply unavoidable, several readers wrote to me to complain that I had ruined the plot of *Anna Karenina* for them. To which I can only say this: Guys. It was published in 1878. There have been eighteen films, nine operas, and five ballets based on this novel, and everyone knows about the train. Get with the program.

Of course, I feel bad. And in an ideal world, we would be able to discuss classics without revealing crucial details of plot and character that might spoil a first reading. But you can't have everything, and I have had to make a choice in writing about these books. I decided that it's better to be open and straightforward than second-guess what readers may or may not already know.

In any case, the good thing about French novels is that plot is far less relevant than it is in the great classics of, say, Russian and English literature. Often the plot of a French novel is obvious from the outset. And it's not about *what* happens. It's about *how* it happens and *why*. This is exactly why these books are so rich in life lessons: they examine why we make the decisions we do and why the psychology of an individual forces them to take a certain path at a certain time. So it is not going to kill you to find out that the girl in *L'Amant* does not get married to the lover; that Emma Bovary does not live happily ever after; and that—however dangerous their liaisons might seem—the Vicomte de Valmont and the Marquise de Merteuil are not going to get it on, no matter how much we want them to. I know these reveals will annoy some readers, but I beg indulgence here because I think there is simply no way to discuss these books openly and usefully without being clear about what happens in them. Think of the spoilers like a pedestrian carrying a briefcase across a Parisian street: it's better to know what's coming than to look away.

1. Don't judge yourself for being young and foolish: *Bonjour Tristesse* by Françoise Sagan

(Or: Interfering in your father's love life can have dire consequences)

FRANÇOISE SAGAN'S supremely indifferent expression as she plowed her car into someone's briefcase without really even noticing was the moment that cemented my longing for France and Frenchness. And it motivated me to seek out Sagan's work and *Bonjour Tristesse*, her 1954 bestseller, written when she was seventeen, published when she was eighteen, an international bestseller by the time she was nineteen. This book went on to sell five million copies worldwide and was translated into twenty-two languages. Beat that, J. K. Rowling! (Actually, the Harry Potter series has sold five hundred million copies and is available in over eighty languages. But that didn't take two months to write when J. K. was seventeen.) The happiness lesson of this book? To be young is a wonderful thing. But you rarely realize that when you are young. I am avoiding writing, "Youth is wasted on the young." My grandmother used to say this often and wistfully, and it always irritated me. It's true. But it's of no help to know this when you are young.

Sagan exemplifies the idea of youthful indifference. I came to think of my screen memory of Sagan's daredevil driving as *"Le Grand Bof,"* the careless driver's version of *La Grande Bouffe*, the 1973 film about a group of friends who planned to eat themselves to death. Françoise Sagan was, I decided, the queen of *"bof"* in a country where you are liable to hear the word *"bof"* several dozen times a day. You will not find *"bof"* in a dictionary. For anyone who has not heard a French person say *"bof,"* it is basically an utterance that can mean anything from "I just don't care" to "No one in the entire world cares" or "I care so little that I don't even acknowledge the existence of the idea of caring." It is the supreme proclamation of dis-regard. In a restaurant it can mean "We don't have any fries left, and we don't have to justify to you why that is." (*Bof.*) In a relationship it can mean "I don't care whether you live or die." (Eh *bof.*) And in the case of Sagan, it can mean "Did I just nearly run that man over with my car? Oh, who cares." (Triple *bof.*) Being able to say *"bof"* sometimes—or even quite a lot of the time—is the key to a good life. I liked Sagan principally because she was 100 percent *bof.* There's a lightbulb that goes on for lots of us at different times of our lives: the moment of inspiration that ties you to a place or an identity. For some people it comes through literature or a wonderful meal or a glass of wine or the feeling that a beautiful piece of music gives you. Or it comes through your admiration of a person who is ambivalent about road traffic accidents.

Bonjour Tristesse is a novel about a teenager whose life takes a disastrous path when she leaves Paris for the summer. Being the living incarnation of that certain kind of dangerous joie de vivre became a charm and a curse for Sagan. Writing in the *New Yorker* in 1998, Sebastian Faulks, a British novelist, described Sagan as portraying "an idealized version of French living." This was easily one of the reasons for the critical and commercial success of *Bonjour Tristesse*, whose tone played as well abroad as it did at home. This was a novel about a beautiful seventeen-year-old girl having sex on (or at least near) the beach in the South of France in the sunshine. Who doesn't like the idea of that? And it wasn't written by some dirty old man. It was written by an actual seventeen-year-old girl. Because of Sagan's youth and her looks (and, let's be honest, her gender)—plus the fact that the novel was fun and sexy—the writer-as-personality became the focus rather than the writing. It was soon a well-known trope that if you asked French people in a survey, "Who is Françoise Sagan?" they would reply that she was a film star. Through no fault or design of her own, she became a celebrity first and foremost. Sagan said, "In 1954 I was being asked to choose between two roles: the scandalous writer or the bourgeois schoolgirl. I was neither of those things. I would rather have been a scandalous young girl and a bourgeois writer." She went on to say that at the time she decided to do the only thing she could think of: just do whatever she wanted. For her this meant taking it "too far," embracing excess.

One area where she could be safely and harmlessly excessive was in the way that she used language, and she frequently teased journalists and interviewers by giving them the outrageous sound bites they craved and then later completely contradicting herself. This is a woman who gave good quote: "A dress makes no sense unless it inspires men to want to take it off you." "Money may not buy happiness, but I'd rather cry in a Jaguar than on a bus." Sometimes this was in jest or self-mockery. Sometimes it revealed perhaps more than she intended. When she was asked to write an obituary for her own life, she wrote: "Her death was a scandal only for herself." Is there anything sadder than that?

It's hard to read about Sagan's life without imagining her as some sort of caricature. You have to wonder (as we will see later with Marguerite Duras and Colette, two other female writers who became twentieth century "brands") where the private person ended and where the "writer-created-for-public-consumption" began. And whether these two selves ended up merging into something unrecognizable. Turning writers into "personalities" is a hallmark of every culture, but I remember being surprised to discover, when I first began to understand conversations in French about celebrities and authors, quite how gossipy the French were. I had been led to understand that the British were the absolute worst for this kind of thing, and so I was shocked to find that the French were just as gripped as everyone back home by tales of dissolute behavior, drugs, adultery, and dying from dropping your hair dryer in the bath. This was one of the first big tests of my French, where my pen pal explained to me who Claude François was: *"Mais comment ça se peut? Tu ne connais pas Claude François? Il est mort dans sa baignoire."* "How can that be? You don't know who Claude François is? He died in the bath." This always stood out to me as a lesson in what people become famous for. Claude François was not introduced to me as an accomplished singer and national treasure; he was introduced to me as a man who had died in the bath. Truly the French are just as bad as the rest of us.

I can see, though, why anyone might confuse Sagan with a fictional character or a movie star. After all, she encouraged this, really. There is a thin line between Françoise, the carefree, fun-loving young woman who wrote a novel, and Cécile, the carefree, fun-loving antiheroine who, from the first page of *Bonjour Tristesse*, is obsessed with the distinction between happiness and sadness. "In the summer in question I was seventeen and perfectly happy." Later on, sadness is seen as an emotion so distant and unlikely that it is "strange" and "new." Cécile is the first-person narrator of the story. She is spending the summer with her father, Raymond, in the South of France, where they've rented a villa. Cécile and Raymond have an unusual relationship: Cécile's mother died when she was young, and Raymond has pretty much left her to her own devices. She harbors very little resentment about this. This aspect is the only part of this novel that did not ring true for me. Although I guess Cécile is in denial about a lot of things, so she might as well be in denial about the fact that her father has behaved pretty irresponsibly toward her. In fact, maybe this is the whole point of the novel, this refusal to see who or what is really to blame for things.

Also present is her father's mistress, Elsa, who is only about ten years older than Cécile. The two seem fond of each other but not overly close. Elsa comes across as someone Cécile finds vaguely amusing and a bit stupid. Suddenly—and unexpectedly—Anne arrives. Anne is an old family friend who knew Cécile's mother. She attempts to treat Cécile in a maternal, reproachful way, and Cécile is not keen on this. It's soon clear, though, that Anne has designs on Raymond and is not going to let Elsa get in the way. Anne is very self-possessed and is—crucially—a fashion designer, so she knows how to dress in order to win a man away from a younger rival. This is how I read it, anyway. I imagine Anne as very pouty and hair-flicky in an Anne-Bancroft-as-Mrs.-Robinson kind of way. Elsa didn't stand a chance.

Raymond and Anne announce their engagement, and Elsa storms off. Cécile is appalled, especially when Anne starts lecturing her about the relationship she has with Cyril, her summer boyfriend (who she's having sex with, thereby preventing any studying, although to be fair, sex or no sex, it's pretty unlikely Cécile would do any studying anyway). Cécile grows so annoyed by Anne's interventions, and the prospect of how much worse they'll get when they return to Paris as a "family," that she hatches a plan. Cécile finds Elsa and persuades her to seduce Raymond again. She makes sure Anne sees them meeting up. Anne is horrified and drives off. Later—massive spoiler alert—Raymond and Cécile find out over the last few paragraphs of the book that she has been killed in a car crash.

What's really interesting is that for some novelists, the conclusion would actually be the start of a novel—the aftermath of an incident that has had an unforeseen outcome. This is the breathtaking chutzpah of this novel, that perhaps only a very young (and arrogant?) person could have written: it carries you along in a haze of cigarette smoke, early-evening glasses of wine, and the aroma of sunscreen on warm skin and then drops you from the top of a cliff and leaves you for dead. Sagan does to the reader exactly what fate (or Cécile?) does to Anne.

Is it a betrayal? Or is it what we were hoping for all along? After all, isn't Cécile's insouciant approach to life insufferable? Why does she get to be so happy when she really isn't that nice of a person? Ultimately the conclusion is ambivalent. You could argue that Cécile has got her comeuppance for not caring about anything: she will surely spend the rest of her life haunted by her actions and by this event. Or you could argue that it won't affect Cécile at all (I do think she will at least smoke a bit more heavily) and that the only person who has suffered is Anne, the most likable—and most caring and innocent—character in the book. Or you could argue that no one is wrong and no one is right. Cécile could have been more caring and less calculating and Anne would still have ended up driving off a cliff. The question you are left asking is "How do we live with the suffering we may have caused?"

The lesson about youth is key even if it's an ambivalent one. Perhaps Cécile is protected by her youthful idiocy: she can pretend that it's OK because she never liked Anne that much anyway. Or perhaps the ending represents the shattering of her youth. It's in the moments running up to Anne's death that we see the idyllic nature of Cécile's existence: she can do what she likes, be whoever she likes, and to hell with the consequences. She doesn't even realize how good she had it until it's too late. This is a common theme in French quotes about happiness. There's a famous line by Jacques Prévert, a poet who was a contemporary of Paul Éluard (the one whose words inspired the title of *Bonjour Tristesse*): "I recognize happiness by the sound that it makes upon departure." Or as someone else once said without having to be a giant of French poetry, "You don't know what you've got 'til it's gone."

In literary terms, this novel asks another question—and it's one that, I think, influenced the reception of *Bonjour Tristesse* and the furor around it: "Is it OK for a novelist to be ambivalent about a terrible incident?" Sagan leaves it for us to judge whether Anne's death is a random accident, a suicide, or something close to manslaughter. Or perhaps it's an unfortunate combination of all three? Sure, Cécile does not explicitly cause her death, but you could argue that she created all the conditions that led up to it. It doesn't seem as if the ending is really about happiness in life, in fact quite the opposite. But it does ask a profound question: "Who is responsible for our happiness?" Cécile attempts to control too much of her own happiness and will leave nothing to chance. She attempts to engineer the fate of her father and of Anne. And she fails disastrously, surely creating a situation that will have consequences for the rest of her life. She's going to end up feeling worse about Anne's death than she ever would have felt if Anne had become her stepmother? Somehow Sagan creates an atmosphere where judgment is suspended. We forgive Cécile for her attempts at massaging fate. She was young. What else was she supposed to do?

Interestingly, although Sagan has always been described as someone who writes brilliantly about the folly of youth (and *Bonjour Tristesse* is one of the best coming-of-age novels ever written), her portraits of people in early middle age are also spot-on. The characters Sagan writes about represent the quintessential Frenchness *d'un certain âge* (of a certain age—i.e., middle-aged) and I observed this for myself when I first spent time in France in the late 1980s. People in their forties and fifties seemed younger than people of that age in the UK. They worried more about what they looked like. Women blow-dried their hair. Everyone smoked. I once saw an extremely chic Frenchwoman, an aunt of my friend, completely lose her mind because her pack of Gitanes went missing off the mantelpiece for about thirty minutes. I learned this lesson: if you're French, even when you become quite old, you are still allowed to behave like a spoiled brat from time to time. Petulance keeps you young.

Described as "a vulgar, sad little book" in a review in the *Spectator* magazine in 1955, *Bonjour Tristesse* was written when Sagan was still at school; in fact, she said she wrote it when she was supposed to be studying. She called it "a simple story about a girl making love with a boy, surrounded by certain complications." She said later that she had told all her friends that she was writing a novel—when she wasn't—and that "by lying about it, I ended up writing." She sent a manuscript to two publishing houses. Éditions Julliard responded by sending a telegram, as her telephone was broken: "Call Julliard urgently." She went into the office, they made her an offer, she drank a large glass of cognac. She had to assure the publisher that "there was no kind of sinister story like that in my own life" (i.e., that she wasn't libeling any adulterers in her family) and that the novel was not autobiographical. Although, as she said later, "Is there any other kind of novel?" Her mother's response upon learning that her daughter was now officially a writer: "It would be better if you could come down for dinner on time and brush your hair occasionally." Her father just laughed.

In *Le Figaro*, François Mauriac, thought of by many as France's greatest living writer at the time, called her "a charming little monster." She soon came to resent her infamy and the idea of *"le phénomène Sagan, le mythe Sagan"* (the Sagan phenomenon, the Sagan myth): "Everyone wants to be thought of as a normal person, to be spoken to normally and not be repeatedly asked whether you like noodles or some other banal nonsense." Sagan said she found the interest in her difficult and that "the photographers were appalling." She particularly resented being expected to recycle amusing anecdotes in interviews. As a result, she kept her mouth shut and acquired a reputation for being sad, which she wasn't at all.

To be fair to the public and press of the time, it must have been difficult to know what to make of Françoise Sagan. The novel itself is unusual and subversive, even sixty-five years after it was written. It is a portrait of a strangely amoral, self-interested universe but one that is hard to judge and seems peculiarly seductive, perhaps because we can all remember what it is like to be a self-obsessed teenager who thinks that they know it all. It is a spectacularly beautiful novel and survives multiple rereadings (not least because it is a very quick read). When we become adults, we realize how silly we were at that age, but I think we also slightly regret not being able to hang on to the determination and blind self-belief of that age. The true attraction of Sagan's narrator, seventeen-year-old Cécile, is that she is a hedonist: she does what she wants, to please herself. She knows it, and she's OK with it: "My love of pleasure and happiness constitutes the only consistent aspect of my character." This is why I take the title of the novel as ironic, playful, or even a bit sick. *"Bonjour tristesse"* is a pose for Cécile. In truth, nothing gets in her way. It's not even clear if Anne's death will puncture her love of pleasure and happiness.

I love how plain-talking Françoise Sagan is as a novelist. When she speaks through Cécile, she is a real bitch. Cécile, for example, considers her father to be a bit of an idiot because he disdains ugliness. The consequence of this is that he ends up hanging out with stupid people a lot. Because, Sagan suggests, beauty and intelligence do not go hand in hand. I often wonder if we are supposed to infer something about the low intelligence—and therefore high beauty—of her father's companion Elsa when we find out that she has come to the South of France at the height of summer without any sunscreen and therefore is red and peeling within days. Cécile on Elsa: "She had, to her credit, done the best she could with her dried-out hair and sunburnt skin but the result was not brilliant. Fortunately she did not seem to realize this."

There's something almost close to the psychopathic portrait of Patrick Bateman in *American Psycho* in *Bonjour Tristesse*. Cécile says that she only cares about happiness, but she also seems to observe psychological states as if from a distance, almost as if they're a pantomime for her. On Anne and Raymond: "They were both smiling and looking happy. I was impressed by that. Happiness has always seemed to me to be a validation, to represent a successful outcome." Sometimes she seems to be parroting the thoughts and feelings of others: "She was gradually going to make of us the husband and daughter of Anne Larsen, which meant that we would become civilized, well-mannered, happy people. For she would make us happy."

So it's clear that to some extent this is an amoral book. It's hard, though, to read it as immoral or shocking. One of the most recent translations of *Bonjour Tristesse* (Penguin Modern Classics, I am looking at you) gleefully informs us that "explicit sexual scenes" were removed from the first English language edition when it came out. But now the "uncensored text" can appear "in full." Exciting! Except guess what, it isn't. I can't even begin to guess what the censored bits were. Yes, it's clear that this seventeen-year-old girl has sex with her boyfriend, the unfortunately named Cyril. But there is no explicit description of sex and really nothing here is any racier than Flaubert describing Madame Bovary's carriage rocking back and forth as it bounces across the paving stones of Rouen.

A side note on Cyril, who despite his name is a superb character in the novel. But why does he have to be called Cyril? Cyril is clearly not a weird name to French people, for some reason. I don't know how it is in American English, but it is not a hot name in British English. It's reminiscent of the line in *When Harry Met Sally* when Harry talks about Sheldon: "A Sheldon can do your income taxes. If you need a root canal, Sheldon's your man. But humpin' and pumpin' is not Sheldon's strong suit." I feel that Cyril shares the same problem as Sheldon. But clearly Françoise Sagan disagrees, and I have to guess that she knows way more about sexy French men than I do.

If this novel feels autobiographical and intimately observed, it's hard not to look at Sagan's family and wonder if it is about them. Clearly, the plot and the circumstances are invented. But the tension and the discomfort are not. I'm afraid to say that there is plenty to suggest that Françoise Sagan's family were unbearable. I suspect she was too. She was born Françoise Quoirez in Cajarc in the Lot in southwest France. The name "Sagan" emerged when she told her father that she wanted to publish *Bonjour Tristesse* and he said that he wouldn't allow it to be published under her family name. She was reading Proust at the time and saw the words "the Duc de Sagan passed by in his carriage."

Her family is usually described as rich and bourgeois. She was born to Pierre, an industrialist whose family had made their money in the north of France, and Marie Laubard, whose family owned land in the south. Françoise was born in 1935 and is often described as "the third child." In fact she was the fourth. Her sister, Suzanne, was born in 1924. Her brother Jacques in 1927. But before Françoise's birth, another boy, Maurice, died in infancy. Years, later when Suzanne was interviewed, she said that Françoise's birth, after the loss of the baby boy before, was seen as a miracle and that she was allowed to do whatever she wanted. This does seem to explain a lot. Sagan herself said later that she was "very happy, very spoiled, and at the same time very solitary" as a child.

In the interview collection *Je Ne Renie Rien*, featuring collected interviews from 1954 to 1992, Sagan lays it all out: "If I had to start all over again, I would start over by avoiding certain minor incidents: car accidents, hospital visits, broken love affairs. But I don't disown any of it." *"Je ne renie rien"*—"I renounce nothing"—has a religious ring to it, as one of the main things you might be called upon to *"renier"* is Satan. It contains the suggestion that Sagan takes full responsibility for all her Satanic deeds. She continued to be productive, writing over forty novels, as well as essays and plays. Although the legendary car crash in 1957—the one that featured all the broken bones mentioned in the TV interview—didn't kill her, it weakened her. This was the one accident she never quite recovered from, and she held it responsible for her use of pills, tranquillizers, alcohol, and drugs.

There's an interesting point to be made here about the intersection of literature and celebrity. Françoise Sagan was perhaps the harbinger for the modern obsession with fame and how it might come to affect writers. There's a narrative that has grown up around the idea of pride coming before a fall for writers who experience success very early in their careers. This is why the section on the latter part of her life is described mournfully in her French Wikipedia entry as *"une fin désenchantée"* ("a disenchanted ending"). In the early 2000s she was convicted of tax fraud and was given a one-year suspended jail sentence. She died of a pulmonary embolism in 2004 at the age of sixty-nine.

One obituary described her as an "impulsive, indulged" child, which to me seems like the best (the only?) kind of child to be. If you cannot be impulsive and indulged when you are a child, when can you be? What matters is whether you continue that behavior as an adult. And when this is mentioned in her obituary, I think what they are trying to say is that she very much did continue this behavior into adulthood. One story has the police searching her home for cocaine. Her dog pointed the way to the cocaine and start licking it. She said, "See? He likes it too." One account claimed that her pet fox terrier overdosed just from sniffing her handkerchiefs. I suspect this is Sagan herself suggesting this, as a joke. In fact, probably all these stories come from Sagan, where she is mocking herself for her addictions.

Sagan once explained that she sees the bright side of things because she cultivates a sense of humor. That whenever she watches a film about Joan of Arc (who—spoiler alert—gets burned at the stake), every time she thinks, "Oh, she'll get out of it somehow." And she thinks the same thing, she used to say, about Romeo and Juliet. She is one of life's optimists, even when it comes to the stories with a foregone tragic conclusion. I'm not sure her life was particularly easy. But it was not a disaster either, despite the Aston Martin smash being the first of many car accidents. Sagan was given a lot of leeway to live the life that she wanted to live, to do—as she had intended—whatever she wanted. As Clive James puts it in the documentary, "A French writer is a national treasure. A female French writer would be forgiven anything."

In truth, Sagan was just like the rest of us. She was once asked something on a television program that stayed with her. "If you had an eighteen-year-old daughter, would you want her to live the same life?" She decided that if she had a daughter—she had one child, a son, by her second husband—her wish for her would be that she would fall in love with a man at the age of eighteen, he would fall in love with her, and the two of them would die together at the same time at the age of eighty, holding hands. "Is there a better romantic idea? But the sadness of life is that in general it is so unromantic that it's very rare for anything like this to happen. People break away from each other. Or something breaks inside them."

Sagan represents the expression of the kind of happiness that is reminiscent of the Leonard Cohen quote about there being a crack in everything. ("That's where the light gets in.") It's not perfect or unbroken, but it's real. This is the French version of happiness, Sagan-style: being young—or stubbornly young at heart—and not caring that you're not appreciating your youth. It's about living in the moment, living for today, sucking the marrow out of life before serving the marrow alongside a side order of the spinal cord of a young calf. I once nonchalantly ordered this dish by accident in a restaurant in the Dordogne and only discovered what it was when I got home and looked it up in the dictionary. Amazingly, I wasn't sick. But I did have terrible dreams about mad cow disease. I am horrified to report that it actually tasted really nice.

Sometimes youthful folly has its rewards, as Cécile would happily tell you, even with the sound ringing in her ears of her future stepmother's car clattering down a cliff. *Bonjour Tristesse* is a deceptive and clever novel. Sagan was perhaps not entirely in charge of its message when she wrote it. It just poured out of her when she was seventeen, and she did not judge Cécile. She neither blames her nor absolves her for her actions. She paints Cécile's life that summer as honestly as she can, never disguising how blissful it is despite the horror around the corner. The horror itself is ambiguous: it might have happened anyway. And it doesn't remove the joy. Perhaps we should all judge ourselves a little less and concentrate harder on clinging to the bliss?

2. When memories visit you, soak them up: *À La Recherche du Temps Perdu* by Marcel Proust

(Or: Find excuses to eat your favorite cake)

THE FREEDOM AND SELF-POSSESSION of Sagan's seventeen-year-old narrator, Cécile, feels, I think, familiar to readers brought up in the English language tradition. We all know what teenage self-abandon—or the promise of it—feels like. We know all about first-person narrators in coming-of-age novels. But there is also something particularly French about this character and the way she experiences the world: the feel of the sun on her skin, she way she watches cigarette smoke curl upward, how she describes a sip of wine. Sagan's calling card is the deliberate evocation of youth. And that feels familiar to all of us. Proust's calling card is something unusual and subjective: involuntary memory. In moments when Proust lost himself in reverie, he was known to push his moustache between his lips and nibble on it. We all have our own versions of this: the expression we pull when we're concentrating or the look in our eyes when we remember something unexpected. This is the big takeaway from Proust: Never mind youth, never mind nostalgia. The real joy to be found in life is in the moments when we forget ourselves and are involuntarily transported back to another time and place. It's an extraordinary trick of time travel that we visit upon ourselves without meaning to and that we can't do by concentrating. It's something that happens when it happens, without us being able to influence it. He celebrates the moments when we are taken outside ourselves without meaning to be.

For me, the idea of a Cécile-type French summer is what people now call a kind of "Proustian" memory. I only have to smell the smoke from a certain kind of cigarette or chew on a plastic straw bobbing in an aluminum can (this is my nibbly moustache) and I'm transported back to the summers that I spent in the company of young French women—not unlike Cécile—in the prime of their youth. They were very different to me in a way: self-possessed, a bit wild, old before their time but not in a jaded way. And—boy, oh, boy—did they have great bodies. And could they tan! These girls were like gorgeous female walnuts made flesh, if the walnuts were shaped like Pamela Anderson in early 1990s *Baywatch*. I was gawky, a bit overweight, stupidly innocent, and the human version of a lobster. A lobster whose flesh audibly sizzled at the faintest hint of a ray of sunshine. I was deeply un-chic and naive, compared to these girls who wore their hair in chignons and, on nights out, drank a sort of pink beer cocktail called *"un Monaco"* (lager with grenadine syrup). The height of my sophistication was knowing to ask for *"un chocolat"* (a hot chocolate) rather than *"un chocolat chaud"* (accurate but marks you out as a foreigner). The setting on those beaches on the Atlantic coast—Pornic, Pornichet, La Baule—is like something out of a Breton version of *Bonjour Tristesse*. But the feelings I have toward it all come straight out of *À La Recherche du Temps Perdu*. Because if you're going to be in search of lost time, isn't that the time you would most want to recapture?

There's a wonderful duality in Proust's lesson in happiness. On the one hand, it's an escape from the present, a quest to seize something that has already disappeared. And yet, it's impossible to do this without being wholly present in the moment. It's a strange kind of supernatural meditation that he seems to be after. When you allow yourself to float into the past on the wave of something you can barely sense in the present. Proust is a fascinating and unique writer in the way that he has inspired an activity that actually has nothing to do with reading: he encourages us to be aware of involuntary memory. To experience involuntary memory—suddenly, unexpectedly, without trying to remember—is one of the most joyous things that can happen to us. This particular memory, dating from the time I first found out about Proust, does not come back to me often, but when it does, it's magical. I spent a couple of summers on the beach with the friends of my French pen pal, a mixed group of boys and girls, between sixteen and nineteen. We lay on the beach (the French girls always topless, me never), smoked a million Philip Morris Light cigarettes (with so little tobacco in them that they were basically paper), and drank cans of Orangina.

The girls were called things like Nathalie, Sandrine, and Mercedes. Mercedes was a name I encountered frequently in France and Spain in the late 1980s and early 1990s, and I always found it hilarious. To me, born as I was, the daughter of a man who owned a modest Ford Cortina, it was like calling yourself Ferrari. All the French and Spanish girls I met with this name styled it out beautifully, though, like heroines from a Pedro Almodóvar movie. Their male friends were called things like Guillaume, Hervé, and Christophe. There was even one called Cyril (he did not cure my aversion to the name), who wore peach V-neck sweaters, had sad, hooded eyes and a very twitchy nose, and was nothing like the sun-kissed Romeo depicted in *Bonjour Tristesse*. He was slightly built and would not feel anything like a dead horse if he were on top of you. Maybe a dead pigeon. Which is somehow even less sexy.

You might think that with my name I'd fit right in with this group. But no. I was not named after an intriguing obscure French poetess nor was I even a misspelling of Vivien Leigh. Although I think I might start telling people that now that I've thought of it. No, none of those beautiful references can be truthfully claimed. I was told that I was named after the wife of the Scottish golfer Sandy Lyle. (As well as owning a Ford Cortina in the 1970s, my parents were—and are—seriously into golf. We must never speak of this.) Years later I realized this could not possibly be true, as Sandy Lyle was fifteen years old when I was born. Later on, he went on to marry women called Jolande and Christine, who would have fit right in at the beach at Pornic. But the point is this: my name is Vivienne, which sounds French, but French people think it is ridiculous. They say Viviane or Vivianne. This is a completely different name. I had to either be friends with pedants, who pronounced my name "Vivienne" in a very ostentatious "I-know-what-I'm-doing" kind of way, or I had to be friends with people who would not learn to say my name correctly and called me Viviane, which sounded so alien to me that I frequently forgot what my name was supposed to be and did not respond to it. Neither option was attractive. Still, I cannot complain, as my name is distinctive, and it has also given me a lifelong empathy for people with unusual names—and a feeling of a secret, inner, slightly misspelled Frenchness. Names are important. Neither of my parents went to university or can speak a foreign language, and they gave me a foreign name possibly with some kind of future progression in mind, or at least a life that would be different to their own—a statement of intent. And it kind of worked.

In Proust, names are particularly crucial, as they denote changes in status over time in a novel where the passing of time is the most important thing. They're also key to understanding Proust simply because there are so many of them. He must have spent ages just thinking them all up. This was further complicated by the fact that many of them have to be heavily (and not-so-heavily) disguised, as they are based on real-life people. In his life, as in his work, names were everything. Names signified social status and a person's lot in life as they moved up and down the ladder. According to one of the most exhaustive websites, Le Fou de Proust, there are 2,511 characters in the novel, all individually listed online in alphabetical order for easy reference, from Abbé (du Mont-Saint-Michel) to Zurlinden (Général Émile August Françoise). In real life, even Proust was not known by his own name: he was christened Valentin Louis Georges Eugène Marcel Proust. His mother called him "little wolf." "Lecram" ("Marcel" backward) was the name that he liked to use with his friend Antoine Bibesco. Weirdly and significantly, given Proust's obsession with names, the name of the narrator—Marcel—does not appear until volume five of *À La Recherche du Temps Perdu*, and even then it is given only as a suggestion of what the narrator's name might be, if he were to share the same name as the author of the book. Possibly the most meta character name suggestion ever. Well done, little wolf.

When I mention volume five, that's not the half of it, although it is more than halfway through the "novel" (actually seven novels). And this is where we come to the big stumbling block with Proust: most people run away because there is just so much of him. When I was studying French literature at university, Proust was seen as the biggest challenge on the reading list. I seem to remember finding it incredibly strange that students of German could take a class uniquely devoted to one writer: Goethe. Similarly, I'm pretty sure that in the English department, Shakespeare would stand on his own. You would not just lump him in with other writers. On my university course, Proust, however, sat alongside dozens of other authors amid "twentieth-century French literature," while our tutors seemed to willfully ignore the fact that Proust had written more words than all of the other authors put together. Proust's output rivals that of Balzac in the nineteenth century. Although, to be fair, word for word Balzac outwrites everyone. But arguably Proust's reputation, the sheer size of him as a literary giant, has outshone Balzac's by a long shot. If you Google the words "Who is the most famous French writer?" then Proust comes in easily in pole position. (Jules Verne, Rousseau, Voltaire, Zola, Racine, and the Marquis de Sade all feature highly in such lists and have all been routinely ignored by this book, for which I can only apologize. Nothing against them.)

When one of the authors on your reading list has written a novel that is over 3,200 pages long (much longer in translation), it's stressful. Even if he were the only author on the reading list, this would be stressful. I have only really been able to read Proust at all by dipping into him intermittently over the past twenty-five years and reading around the novel with biographies and essays. I know people who have spent three years reading the entire thing in sequence. I suspect it can be read in a lot shorter time if you are truly committed. The author Gretchen Rubin has blogged extensively about taking on Proust as a summer reading project. But knowing myself as a reader, I'm not sure how much of it I would really take in if I tried to read it any faster.

In a way, it's tricky with Proust because we are encouraged to take that seven-volume work as a whole. But in reality, it's like reading the whole of Shakespeare end to end. Which is not a fun summer reading project. Shakespeare's complete works total around eight hundred thousand words. That is less than *À La Recherche du Temps Perdu*. So my suggestion to you is this: break it up into chunks, dip in, and/or let yourself off the hook. I always think that Proust would rather you experience your own memories than read everything he wrote. Let me state this clearly: no one would expect you to have read every single word that Shakespeare ever wrote in order to be able to enjoy and discuss *Hamlet*. So why feel the same way about Proust? It is enough to have read one or two of the seven novels or at least to have delved into the "madeleine" chapter and read a biography.

By taking a non-completist stance on Proust, you are in good company. I don't know if I am even allowed to reveal this, twenty-five years later, but a sympathetic tutor took pity on us at university and told us that it was OK if we read only the first and last volumes of *À La Recherche du Temps Perdu*. This was said as a whispered aside in passing, and I hesitate to admit it even now, as I don't want to get this kind soul into trouble. Anyway, it was good advice, as this is how I got through this "book" (or at least two-sevenths of it), and I seem to remember that I decided to overreach by also reading some (all?) of *The Guermantes Way* (volume 3) just because I liked the title. I must have rejected volume 2 completely purely on the grounds of hating the title. (*In the Shadow of Young Girls in Flower*. Proust!

What were you thinking?) Years later I was horrified to realize that the last three volumes were in any case not completely signed off on by Proust and were pieced together by his brother from fragments. So, really, it would have made more sense to read the first two novels rather than the first and the last. But anyway, it's too late now. That, then, is my heathen's recommendation. Read the first and last volumes. Unless you must be a completist, in which case be my guest; over a million words are waiting for you.

With Proust you have license to read selectively, I think, because his attitude to plot is hardly conventional. In short: you don't miss anything. There is no real plot and no real ending and, in any case, it was never properly finished by Proust, so you could argue that he might not have wanted it to be published in this state anyway. No, the real reason to read the first and last volumes is that it will help you to stay in love with Proust, intrigued by him and slightly mesmerized, without being crippled by the realization that he has dominated your entire life. And if you are thinking, "This is disgraceful. Everyone must read the entire thing" (without having done this yourself), then please bear in mind that I am revealing what is advised to University of Cambridge students who have devoted their lives to the study of French and who speak the language fluently. I'm just trying to get more people who wouldn't usually want to read any Proust to read a bit of Proust.

If you cannot face reading any of it at all, let me attempt the impossible and précis *À La Recherche* in five sentences. The narrator spends the first forty pages remembering what it was like to wait for his mother to come and kiss him good night in bed. Over these forty pages—and, in much great detail, over the next seven volumes—fifty years of his life pass before his eyes, filtered through his memory. It's a life filled with friends, family, aristocratic acquaintances, unhappy love affairs, and sudden flashes of tea-soaked cake. In the beginning the narrator is worried that it is impossible to recapture time, but by the end he realizes that time lives on in our unconscious. Oh, I think I might have done it in four sentences. Unfair? Maybe. But not unrealistic. Proust is, I would suggest, an activity, an experience. His writing is like meditation: in order to understand it, you must be immersed in it.

This is the unique thing about Proust: it is just not the same as reading anyone or anything else. In terms of his reputation, he has been transformed into some kind of uber-writer. The romantic, imprecise, impressionistic quality of his writing represents the height of Frenchness. But he also ticks a certain box as a writer's writer (many writers are obsessed with him) and as the twentieth-century ideal of what a writer should be: an eccentric, mercurial genius. Even if you know very little about Proust, you will know that he spent a lot of time in bed, that he wrote a novel that went on for seven volumes and took him thirteen years to write, and that he looked like the cartoon version of an early-twentieth-century writer. Mournful. Curl of hair on the forehead. Twirly moustache. Basically, he's memorable and easy to picture.

Proust as a phenomenon also encompasses two ideas that became hugely important in the second half of the twentieth century. First, he is the writer most closely associated with an almost cinematic or photographic evocation of childhood and memory, particularly through the image of the madeleine. You only have to say the word "madeleine," and a certain number of people who do not speak French will know that you are talking about Proust. Even people who have no real idea of what a madeleine looks like will know that you are talking about Proust. It's a small aromatic sponge cake that looks a bit like a closed seashell. Second, and not unimportant, he is arguably the first prominent world-class writer of the twentieth century to be associated with homosexuality. Proust was not—and could not be—openly gay during his lifetime, but his sexuality was an open secret. His books refer to many gay and bisexual characters. I don't want to say anything quite as crass as "Proust is a gay icon," but whether he would like it or not, essentially he is.

He is also a geek icon. As you can already tell from Proust's inability to let the reader know what the narrator is called until volume five and only suggest very begrudgingly and indefinitely what that name might be, Proust is one of those writers—like Nabokov or Joyce—who attracts the attention, worship, and scrutiny of the sort of people my eight-year-old son would call "brainiacs." Now, I am no slouch in the brainiac department myself, let's not be falsely modest. I can recite several Baudelaire poems by heart, especially if you douse me in enough Sancerre. But Proust . . . Well, he's intimidating. He is the one writer perhaps above all others who attracts the attention of people who want to show off and let you know that they're happy to read a book that actually goes on for seven books.

But Proust is also attractive because there are two Prousts. There is the Proust who belongs to the brainiacs. The writer's writer. No, not even that: the literary critic's writer. This is the Proust whose metaphors and messages can be endlessly examined across his correspondence and his many millions of words. And then there is the one I think of as My Proust (I feel this is a very Proustian appellation, and I'm sticking with it): the one who just wants to stay in bed all day and dream about cakes. This is the kind of Proust that anyone can get on board with. This is the Proust that you can—scandalously—skim-read, rereading the passages you fall in love with and discarding the rest. Do I mean this? Is this sacrilege? Yes. Maybe. But I stand by it. Some would even argue that not only is it the only realistic way to read Proust, it's the way Proust would have wanted. There is a whole school of thought that Proust is less about reading than about rereading: you do not read it once and then say you've read it. You attempt it multiple times. You think of it as similar to a piece of music: you don't hear it once and then let it go. You return to it. You hear things you didn't hear before. You realize there are whole passages you didn't even really register before.

Graham Greene said Proust was the greatest novelist of the twentieth century. Virginia Woolf worshipped the little wolf and said, on reading *À La Recherche*: "Well, what remains to be written after that?" André Gide was haunted by the fact that as a publisher he turned down the first volume of *À La Recherche du Temps Perdu*. In an illustration of how much writers love Proust but how strongly many others are repulsed by him, Edmund White tells the slightly tragic story of novelist Jean Genet in his biography, *Marcel Proust: A Life*. Jean Genet was in prison after a series of arrests for thefts and "lewd acts" (about which I would like to know a whole lot more). One day he was late into the prison exercise yard for the hour when prisoners exchanged books. "He was forced to take the one book all the other prisoners had rejected," White writes. Of course, it was by Proust. In Genet's case, this cast-off novel that no one else could be bothered to read, even in prison, inspired his novel *Our Lady of the Flowers*.

What might Proust, then, inspire in the rest of us? The creation of a great literary work? An explosion of previously forgotten memories? The illumination of the meaning of life? The ultimate expression of happiness? I would be willing to bet that it would inspire in almost anyone a compulsion to Google madeleine recipes. (I recommend sallysbaking addiction.com. You have my blessing to ignore the sites that refer to "French Butter Cakes." Now, that really is sacrilege. They are madeleines! Call them by their name!)

Am I saying that it's more important to know a bit about Proust and have his books on your shelves rather than to actually read him? Perhaps a little. But not too much. He is, however, one of the writers I feel we should be honest about. People do not read his work from start to finish. They just don't. We cannot ignore the tastes of Genet's fellow prisoners. They didn't even want to read Proust when they were in prison and there was nothing else to read. This is one of the reasons Alain de Botton's *How Proust Can Change Your Life* was so popular. De Botton read it all so you didn't have to. Even Anatole France said that Proust's sentences were "long enough to make you consumptive." Now, I'm not going to take things quite as far as Germaine Greer, who once wrote that she would rather visit a demented relative than read Proust. But I tend to agree with her analysis that it's possible that even Proust himself would have regarded reading *À La Recherche du Temps Perdu* as a form of *"temps perdu"* in itself. In other words: don't lose more time looking for lost time.

Greer makes the error, though, of mistaking lost time for wasted time. Proust is not bothered about misspending time. He is interested in recapturing the past. His interest is in revisiting and recalling what has already existed and trying to preserve it. Rather like Nabokov's obsession with memory and "pinning things down" (which became rather literal in the case of his lepidopterology), Proust is on a nostalgic time-traveling quest where his present self travels backward and his past self travels forward, and somehow they meet in the middle. This fusion of time is what gives life meaning. It's a deeply felt understanding of what frustrates so many of us in this life. Does anything really matter? How do we know if it matters? Does what we do affect what happens in the future? This is what joy is for Proust: reconciling the fear of loss with an understanding that nothing is ever completely lost.

Interestingly, this contradictory idea can be sensed in the two warring English translations of the title: *In Search of Lost Time* versus *Remembrance of Things Past*. There's a distance in meaning between these two translations that encapsulates what Proust is trying to do. It also reveals—like magic!—exactly what he's doing that no one has ever really done before. The phenomenon of "involuntary memory" did not exist until Proust brought it into being. The first title—*In Search of Lost Time*—is, I think, a better literal translation, even though it's less poetic. The idea of a search for lost time implies possibility and a quest. It has a sci-fi vibe. It could be a Jules Verne novel with a title like that. But with Proust, we know he's not using the time travel we know about from science fiction. So what other way is there? Within that translated title, there is a sense of the unreal and the unknown. If something is really lost, why would you search for it? You have to believe that it's not really lost and can be found, without using a time machine.

Remembrance of Things Past, however, conjures up something completely different. It suggests almost a commemoration of what has already happened. It implies that memory is fixed and that what happened in the past is fixed. The lesson Proust teaches us is about the direction of travel. We can't really go back in time using our memory. We can only wait for the moments when time travels forward from the past to us and reenters our memory. This happens not because we apply memory to the past ("I want to remember this thing"). It happens because our senses (smell, hearing, taste, in particular, in Proust's case) allow the past back in ("It's coming back to me now").

There is something very wise, almost religious, about this idea. That the past is a place that should be respected: it will visit you when it's ready, not on demand when you want it to. It also encompasses the modern obsession with "mindfulness" and "being present," just as if you try very hard to meditate while you are meditating, you will spoil your own meditation. So if you try very hard to revisit the past, it won't come back to you. The only time we don't seem to struggle with revisiting the past is when we get old and live in it perfectly, because that is where our mind has gone. Old people love getting lost in previous versions of themselves. They are able to remember great swathes of time from formative periods of their lives, even if they can't remember what they had for lunch yesterday or whether they have washed their hair since Sunday.

When Greer says she would rather visit a demented relative than read Proust, I tend to think, "But reading Proust *is* like visiting a demented relative. Only you are the relative." The madeleine itself has something of the vibe of an old people's home about it: when all you have to look forward to is teatime every day, when you are brought your tea and cakes at the same time every day and the only way you can pretend to yourself that the cakes are not that stale is to dunk them in your tea. This is exactly what Proust does with his madeleine. I'm not saying that Proust is someone who acts like he's living in an old people's home that he has created in his own mind (population: one) and then writes a stream-of-consciousness diary of everything he's thinking, but . . . Ah, well, I said it now.

It is fascinating that the concept of the madeleine should be so resonant. I sometimes wonder if Proust just invented "involuntary memory" as cover for cake addiction. ("Oh, I'm just doing my important literary experiments. We're going to have to send out for more madeleines. I can't work without them.") This is something we can all identify with. Annoyingly, though, his experiment worked, and a "madeleine moment" really is a thing. As an idea, there is something about it that is weirdly similar to Andy Warhol's comment about being famous for fifteen minutes. The idea that everyone can have their own version of this kind of sensory transportation has become ingrained in Western culture, even if we don't immediately think of it that way. In some ways, Instagram is like a treasure trove (or a rubbish dump) of narcissistic Proustian moments, fixed in time and preserved forever as a picture, without having to write a word. Imagine if Proust had had Instagram. What would his life have been like? Maybe he would not have written anything. He would have just posted thousands of pictures of his afternoon tea.

The Proustian idea of memory was peculiarly ahead of its time: it's individualistic, cinematic ephemera. And what is more celebrated in our modern age? A random search on Twitter yields dozens of Proustian references over a seventy-two-hour time period, referencing everything from the feel of a LEGO in the hand and colored mascara on the eyelashes to the scent of cleaning fluid and watermelon Jolly Ranchers. This gives you some idea of how pervasive this idea of "Proustian" and "madeleines" is. It is extremely easy to understand; it was an idea that was unconscious in all of us until Proust made it conscious.

I am tempted to argue that there is no other more powerful or better-known abstract idea from literature. This is an extraordinarily profound and beautiful thing and, surely, the one thing any writer dreams of: the ability to excavate a primitive, unspoken feeling that lies deep inside everyone but only becomes obvious when you give words to it. It's a wildly optimistic and thrilling idea and is surely the not-so-secret reason we read books: we hope someone will tell us something about ourselves—and about human existence—that we knew but didn't know. It's that feeling of "Yes! I knew that all along, I just never realized! It's all coming back to me now."

Before we start thinking that Proust is some kind of mystical genius, it's important to remember that the effect of writing is not always intentional. It seems extraordinary that the reputation of one author could rest on a small but perfectly formed sponge creation, but such is life. We must not judge readers for the things that capture their imagination. Proust himself could not have known that this idea in particular would have such resonance, and it was not all perfectly designed. Strangely, this famous passage was arguably very nearly not about madeleines at all. As a 2013 exhibition at the Bibliothèque Nationale de France showed, Proust's manuscripts from 1910 featured the word *"biscottes"* before they featured the word "madeleines." A *biscotte* is such a horrible, terrible thing (savory, dry, almost-burnt toast) that I can't even bear to think of Proust eating one, but I suppose he must have done. It reminds me of Michelle Obama and the *crêpe fromage*. She had the wrong kind of pancake. And yet her Parisian audience still loved her. Proust had the wrong kind of cake. But somehow it still worked out.

Of course, as much as for remembering cakes he ate a long time ago, Proust is known for being miserable and staying in bed the whole time. Indeed, whenever I see a portrait of Proust's face, it makes me think of that Sheryl Crow lyric: "I wonder if he ever had a day of fun in his whole life." The biographer Edmund White describes Proust as growing up in a bedroom which stank of "eucalyptus fumigations" for his asthma. This is where I warm to Proust considerably: I have asthma and had numerous chest infections as a child. I was constantly threatened with "an inhalation to clear everything out." It doesn't make you into a nice person. Proust's mother was so used to his languishing, ill, in bed that she once sent him a questionnaire asking him to fill in what time he had gotten out of bed. I can't help thinking that at least part of his illness and his languishing was to do with how much his mother obsessed over him. Proust's relationship with his mother is at the heart of his work, even though he did not start to write his great work until a few years after her death. The novelist Colm Tóibín once suggested in a review of a Proust exhibition in the *New York Review of Books* that Proust perhaps "had the lovely idea that his mother, by dying, had left an enormous blank for him to fill in. She wanted all the details, she wanted to be spared nothing as she sat on her chair in heaven, her eyes cast down, and he would do anything to please her."

When he was around twenty-six years old, they had a fight relating to a photograph his mother had seen of Proust with his friends Robert de Flers and Lucien Daudet. It was not an indecent photograph, but it caused an argument as to the nature of Proust's romantic inclinations. Flying off into a rage, he slammed a door, which caused panes of glass to shatter. In her letter to him after this incident, she wrote, "Let's think no more and talk no more about it. The broken glass will merely be what it is in the temple—the symbol of an indissoluble union . . ." She added: "PS I do however have to return to the subject in order to recommend that you don't walk without shoes in the dining room because of the glass."

Proust uses this incident in his novel *Jean Santeuil*, and it is frequently analyzed because it reveals not only something about his relationship with his mother but also something about the family's Judaism, which Proust rarely acknowledged (his mother was Jewish): the "union" celebrated by broken glass is a marriage between man and wife. A strange thing to mention at any time, but a particularly strange one to mention in the context of an argument with your son about his homosexuality. No wonder Proust wanted to go and hide under his bedcovers.

People have been very irritated that Proust was not exactly Mr. Gay Pride. (When I say "people," I mostly mean André Gide, who may have been residually angry that he, as a publisher, had turned down *À La Recherche du Temps Perdu*.) Proust never acknowledged that he was gay, and many have argued that he depicted homosexuality as an unpleasant thing. Edmund White writes: "Years later he would tell André Gide that one could write about homosexuality even at great length, so long as one did not ascribe it to oneself." As a young man, Proust was more accepting of his desires, because he believed that homosexuality was not the vice for boys that it was for grown men. It was only when you grew older that it became a problem. He really was the king of euphemisms in this regard, once describing himself as someone who "under the pretext of loving a friend as a father, might actually love him as a woman would."

I'm being unnecessarily mean here because, of course, things were different during Proust's era. And in any case, even in the present day we tell ourselves all kinds of lies about our desires and our identity in order to maintain certain fictions about ourselves. Still, in an era when things were beginning to change, Proust's unwillingness to show the honesty that he clearly prized in other aspects of life marked him out as disingenuous for some during his own lifetime and afterward.

Many critics have said that there is a sense in which Proust "talks" backward and forward. His work is a conversation with the tradition evident in Tolstoy, Flaubert, Zola. But it also projects forward toward the modernism of James Joyce or even the magical realism of Gabriel García Márquez. The writer currently alive who owes the most to him is Karl Ove Knausgaard, Norway's Proust. The essayist and critic Daniel Mendelsohn has written that Knausgaard "shrinks the entire world to the size of the narrator's consciousness." He argues that Proust does almost the opposite: he seeks to extract some kind of personal experience from a huge canvas, in the style of a nineteenth-century novel. He's not wrong. But I think the two writers can be read together and have a similar feel. They're just adjusting their lens in a slightly different way. Where Proust deserves his place in all our hearts is in his willingness to turn himself inside out and download—meticulously—the contents of his brain in order to make the rest of us feel less alone. He's vulnerable, observational, and introspective, creating a lens onto the world that makes us see it in a completely different light. He is the opposite of *bof*. He makes you care. Maybe too much. Although I've got to tell you from bitter experience that this is not a beach read, whether you're topless or not. Proust is like poetry: keep him by your bedside and let him keep you company from time to time. Bed was his favorite place. It's what he would have wanted. You just have to make sure you can get plenty of cake delivered to you there.

This might be a very meta thing to add. And I'm already embarrassing myself just by thinking it. But for me, the experience of reading Proust has become a "madeleine moment" in itself. It happens when I'm reading something else, by another author. It might be something difficult and impenetrable that I'm not quite taking in. Or a piece of poetry that I can understand with my emotions but makes no sense to me intellectually. Or I will be reading a novel before realizing that I have been reading for several pages and I have not understood anything but I am still enjoying the book. And suddenly I will think, "Oh, this is like reading Proust." And it takes me back to the moments when I was first lost in *À La Recherche du Temps Perdu* and feeling exhilarated but also wondering if it was OK to enjoy a book as if it were a piece of music and not really be able to tell anyone what had happened in the pages you had read. Turns out, it is OK. If it's pleasurable and it gives you something, it's OK.

3. Sometimes you've just got to make the most of what you've got: *Gigi* by Colette

(Or: Don't let someone publish your work under the name Willy)

PROUST WAS A celebrity author within his own lifetime—and he wrote masterfully about the horrors and hypocrites of high society. But he took no pleasure in being what the French call "people." This is one of my favorite words and concepts in the French language—except for *bof*, obviously. "People" is the English noun borrowed and turned into an adjective. It is used in French to mean something like "belonging to the in-crowd" or "verging on a celeb." "*Un magazine* people" is a gossip magazine. You might say of a television presenter, "*Elle est très* people" to mean "she's always in the gossip columns." It was first said to me, I think, by a French friend, explaining her opinion of Madonna. "*Bof.*" She shrugged, "*Elle est trop* people." ("Meh. She's too much into being a celeb.") Of all the writers who could be said to be happily "people," Colette is it.

For many years I was ignorant of the existence of Colette, despite having seen the film *Gigi* many times as a child. In fact, one of the songs from the film's soundtrack, "Thank Heaven for Little Girls," formed part of my grandad's "inky-pinky parlez vous" repertoire of things that sounded French but were not French at all. Turns out that even if you sing like Maurice Chevalier in heavily accented English, you are not actually singing in French. *Gigi* formed part of the mid-twentieth-century myth of Frenchness: all nudge-nudge, wink-wink, Folies Bergère. Even as a child I thought this was old-fashioned and a bit odd. It didn't occur to me for a second that this musical hall type of film could be based on a novel written by a rather fascinating woman.

Colette is not someone who was taught on my university syllabus. She wasn't even mentioned. I eventually realized who she was when I saw a repeat of *Gigi*, the 1958 movie, which won an at-the-time record nine Academy Awards. (That record was then promptly broken by *Ben-Hur* the following year.) Instead of being a staple of the academic curriculum for the past fifty years like many of the writers here, Colette is someone who has been ripe for reinvention within the mainstream: as a force of nature, a subversive rule-breaker, and a "feminist icon." I find that expression slightly odd and humiliatingly meaningless, signifying something like "a woman who wasn't supposed to succeed because, er, she was a woman." In many ways Colette was the opposite of what we might call a feminist now. After all, *Gigi*, a novel published in 1944, is basically another take on the *Pretty Woman* story. Take a young woman destined to be a prostitute—or at the very least someone's mistress. Take a man who frequents prostitutes but has a heart of gold. Mix them together over a number of picturesque incidents, and sure enough they will fall in love. The little lady will no longer have to sell herself for money. And the fine gentleman will no longer have to buy love. In theory. In reality, of course, have they merely entered into a long-term, legally sanctioned prostitute-client relationship? Discuss.

Colette is as tricky to analyze as a writer as she is to analyze as a feminist. As a celebrity in the most modern sense and a showbiz character, she is an utter delight, a biographer's and

screenwriter's dream. She was tempted away from an innocent, rural childhood as a child bride for Willy, one of the most
notorious figures of the Paris literary world. Willy was the
pen name of the literary impresario Henry Gauthier-Villars,
who employed a stable of writers to churn out books for his
publishing house. He groomed Colette into one of the most
sought-after figures of his social circle and set her to work as
one of his authors. Between the two of them they created several bestselling sensations of the early twentieth century, with
the Claudine novels (1900–03). She then grew tired of their
association and his control and left him for a woman called
Missy, who dressed as a man. Launching a career onstage
initially with Missy, Colette then forged a path in music halls,
where she showed her breasts, began publishing her own
novels, and even reported from the frontline of World War I.
When her collected works were published in 1948, they ran
to two million words. (I know I keep counting all the authors'
words, but I'm just trying to put across how insanely prolific
these people were in the days before the internet. Just saying.)

Born Sidonie-Gabrielle Colette in Yonne in 1873, Colette
took her unusual name Sidonie from her mother, who was
known as Sido. Colette later acknowledged the debt that she
owed to her mother and was very fond of her. By all accounts
she had a happy rural upbringing, but her family's financial
situation was precarious. At the age of eighteen, Colette
moved in with her brother, and it was around this time that
she met Willy. They were married for seventeen years but were
estranged some of that time—and also together, by all accounts,
occasionally afterward. Willy was responsible for two things:
one, making Colette realize that she could write, and two,
making her realize that she would rather do it without him.

But at first Colette's career began as a ghostwriter. The modern-day equivalent of Willy's writing factory has been cited as James Patterson, the bestselling crime writer who works with a number of co-authors, of which Bill Clinton is one: they wrote *The President Is Missing* together. Willy set the precedent for this kind of thing. Only he was not as transparent about his brand as Patterson, whose collaborations are clearly signaled. Instead Gauthier-Villars would commission a writer and then publish them under a different name, often signing them under his own pen name, as if "Willy" had written everything. He was not keen for the authors themselves to receive any credit, to the extent that he insisted on a particular narrative about the emergence of the Claudine novels: that they just appeared anonymously on his doorstep, as a package tied with pink ribbon. In fact, some of the time he had locked Colette in a room to write them.

As a biographical narrative, then, Colette has got it all, really. Beautiful, exciting, racy, prolific, multitalented. Plus, she is someone who fits very well into the questions of identity and sexuality that our modern age is fascinated by. And in a way that we can talk about and examine openly. This wouldn't have been possible in Colette's day. What concerns me, though, is whether we can really say that she has the literary pedigree to match. As much as I want to be able to insert as many overlooked women writers as possible into the canon of great classics, I don't think it serves feminism or women if we end up adding in names just because they were women. Colette, however, is a phenomenon by any objective measure. It's incredibly useful to measure her impact both as a writer from outside the Paris set, at a time when literature was all about who you knew and what circles you moved in, and, of course, as a woman, and especially as a young woman. Whatever you say about her, she definitely broke the mold, and for that reason alone, her entire life is a lesson in happiness.

Although the Claudine novels were a highlight of Colette's career (a thinly disguised autobiographical series about the coming-of-age of a schoolgirl), it is *Gigi* that she is now most remembered for. It's the sweetest and funniest and most ridiculous read. And it really has aged terribly. When I say funny, I mean unintentionally. It is horrifically archaic and politically incorrect, even for the period in which it was written. In a way there is something almost sad about the fact that this book was written in 1944. Although, yes, it's set at the turn of the century, it somehow feels like something out of a much earlier era. It's almost as if there is a certain kind of writing that Colette wished she could have been doing when she was much younger. But she was unable to do it because she was under Willy's control. By the time these books flooded out of her at a voracious pace, they were really no longer reflective of the period and certainly no longer reflective of her as a person nor of the life she was living. *Gigi* is part of a series of Colette books that were sort of written after they should have been written.

This is not an easy read for the modern reader, as it is so old-fashioned and unsubtle. Even within the first few pages, Gilberte—Gigi, our fifteen-year-old heroine—is folding her "heron-like" legs underneath her, fussing about her ringlets and parading her "slender calf and high-arched instep." Even without Willy at her shoulder, Colette cannot help including the details that would be thrilling only to early-twentieth-century gentleman readers who enjoy having the leg of a piano described to them in exhaustive detail. (Genuine quote: "You see, Grandmamma, with my skirts too short . . .") It's all rather tiring but also weirdly happy-making in a giddy sort of way. Think: *Little Women* go to the Moulin Rouge. So if the thought of Gigi's fifteen-year-old slim waist and sailor-trim hat on every other page makes you want to hurl, then this is not the novel for you. In parallel with Colette's real-life relationship with Willy, the relationship between Gigi and Gaston is marked by childish nicknames and gifts of licorice. For the modern reader, there is something distinctly creepy about this. And it definitely stands in stark contrast to seeing Colette portrayed as a sort of Virginia-Woolf-meets-suffragette character in the 2018 film starring Keira Knightley as Colette and Dominic West as Willy.

To be fair, the plot is so perennial and predictable that it was indeed still going years later with the movie *Pretty Woman*, released in 1990. Set in turn-of-the-century Paris, Gigi is being groomed for the life of a high-class courtesan when she is "rescued" by a wealthy patron called Gaston. It's *Pygmalion*, *My Fair Lady*, and every book or movie that has tried to make a sentimental story out of exploitation rolled into one. I can't help feeling that without the involvement of the utterly irreproachable Audrey Hepburn in the stage version and Leslie Caron in the movie, *Gigi* might have sunk without a trace.

It's a short book—only sixty pages—and a simple tale. Gigi's family moves in influential circles, and her relatives have befriended a charming playboy called Gaston. He is fed up with life and with chasing after various women who play games with him in an attempt to get him to propose. So he enjoys the supposedly innocent company of Gigi and her companions, where he doesn't have to worry about all that stuff. We are supposed to imagine that Gigi is not "good enough" to be married off to Gaston so he can just relax in her company.

Until one day when Gigi is launched into society and Gaston realizes that she is no longer a child; in fact, she is a beautiful young woman and—get this!—someone he would quite like to marry. Which he does. But not before first attempting to get her to be his mistress. Gigi doesn't stand for this, and so she ensnares him as her husband in the end. Happy days!

There's no way of suggesting that Gigi is some kind of undiscovered masterpiece that should be regarded in the same way as *À La Recherche du Temps Perdu*. But it's a window onto Colette's world and a fascinating take on a kind of feminism that is very different to today's versions. Of course, by the time Colette wrote this, she was past her most scandalous behavior. But there was still something unusual about the way she portrayed things, and even in the 1940s she was still a little ahead of her time. In the story, she tries very hard to give Gigi some agency and spirit, no doubt basing her on herself. Decades later, Gigi's predicament comes across as barbaric, and it seems ridiculous to applaud her for having managed to marry the man who wanted to make her into a kept woman. But within the story, Gigi's behavior is unusual: she knows what she wants, and she knows the fate she wants to avoid. She refuses to be trapped into a life where she is the plaything of a wealthy man with none of the advantages and respectability of marriage. She behaves with some degree of freedom and autonomy and is authentic with Gaston: she tells him that he must take her on her terms or not have her at all. This isn't exactly Gloria Steinem stuff, but for 1940s France—and especially for Colette, who was, I think, trapped in the mentality of a much earlier era—it will have to do.

Maybe I'm mean to harbor suspicions that Gaston is actually just a dirty old man. Gaston's behavior is seen as perfectly understandable and unremarkable, as he is just amusing himself before he gets married. He is thirty-three years old and with a lot of wealth weighing heavily on his shoulders. "Gaston's mistresses have all had an air about them. A liaison with a great professional lady is the only suitable way for him to wait for a great marriage, always supposed that some day he does marry," Colette writes. Yes! The only suitable way! God forbid he might take up a hobby instead of using women as his pastime. But Gaston's point of view—and the entire moral of this story—is important: Gigi is a reminder of how far women's lives have come.

We are not going to squeeze the joy out of Colette via close scrutiny of her plots, then. However, there is Technicolor happiness galore in her work, in her gloriously innocent and life-affirming depictions of the little things—like jewels, for example. As Colette's biographer Judith Thurman points out, jewels and gemstones are important to understanding Colette's world, and they are very much part of Gigi's as well. It's fascinating to me that decades after her association with Willy, Colette is still immersing herself in the transactions between dirty old men and young girls. There is an exchange between Gigi and Aunt Alicia, the retired courtesan who is instructing her, where the aunt is teaching the niece the difference between the stones: which ones are truly valuable and which ones only look as if they are valuable, all the while knowing that she was gifted these jewels as a reward—basically—for being a prostitute. Nonetheless, they represent her self-worth, and she wants it respected.

For Gigi, this is a lecture—a hypocritical one—about knowing your value: "Never wear second-rate jewels. Wait 'til the really good ones come to you." I'm not sure Colette meant it the way it reads nowadays (as she is presumably on Aunt Alicia's side), but the reader sees it as a lecture in knowing the value of everything but the worth of nothing. And this is very much the problem with Colette's legacy. There is an ambiguity about the purity and old-fashioned quality of her work versus the staleness of the themes. Colette's writing has a quality that Thurman calls the "greenness" or "freshness" of voice, which was incredibly unusual in early-twentieth-century literature. "There are touches of the green of poison, the green of acid, the green of bile, but the verdancy of youth is their antidote," writes Judith Thurman. I can agree with this if Colette had written all this around the same time. But she continues to rewrite the same story and breathe the same air years later. There's something tragic about it. For British readers, it has the aura of Barbara Cartland, the romance novelist known for being one of the best-selling authors of the twentieth century (her books have sold 750 million copies). She was an eccentric character who only wore pink well into her nineties, dressing in puffy princess dresses as if she was an overgrown little girl. Cartland was satirized as Dame Sally Markham in the popular British TV comedy *Little Britain*, where she was portrayed as wonderfully camp and monstrous, padding about her country estate in a cerise party gown and dictating her romance novels to her secretary by reading out passages of the Bible.

Even as we were approaching the freedom and the breath of fresh air that was the 1950s, Colette was still writing about courtesan rituals and (really, quite old) men who came round to have "chats" with fifteen-year-old girls in exchange for baubles they could keep in their jewelry box. Thank 'eaven for little girls indeed, to quote Maurice Chevalier's theme song as Honoré, Gaston's uncle, in the film version of *Gigi*.

In the passages in *Gigi* about jewels, knowledge of these things is one measure of a woman's power. Gigi learns that it's important not to be seen to be asking for too much: "These three feminine creatures never asked him for pearls, chinchillas or solitaire diamonds, and they knew how to converse with tact and due solemnity on scandalous topics traditional and recondite." Gigi knows "from the age of twelve" that Madame Otero's string of black pearls were "'dipped'—that is to say artificially tinted," while her other three-string pearl necklace is "real" and worth a lot of money. Her grandmother instructs her to break off a friendship with a girl at school because the girl has been seen wearing a diamond ring given to her by an admirer, and being seen with it in public is tacky (and means the family has less leverage over the man who gave it to the girl). There's no sense, of course, that exposing one's daughter or granddaughter to men who want to give her a solitaire when she is barely a teenager is tacky or weird or ill-advised or anything like that.

It's ridiculous to judge Colette according to modern standards, and she is a brilliant window on the mentality of yesteryear, especially from the point of view of a woman who was desperate to claw some of her own authority and power in a world that was badly weighted against her. On the other hand, though, I feel perfectly comfortable in criticizing Colette the writer for inheriting something of Willy's cynicism: she doesn't move with the times or with any different sense of morality or new cultural standards emerging as the decades pass. She sticks to her turn-of-the-century narrative.

Perhaps even more bizarrely, Colette was in her early seventies when she wrote *Gigi*. I don't want to be too cruel to Colette—and the picture painted of her as a complicated feminist icon in the 2018 movie is an extremely generous and important one—but this period was not her finest hour. Despite the fact that her husband at the time was Jewish and had been arrested by the Gestapo (he was returned within months), she wrote for pro-Nazi newspapers and worked on a novel in the early 1940s that had anti-Semitic references. I'm not a great fan of judging people too harshly for doing what many others were doing at the same time—I take the Camus line that it is better to understand than to accuse—but I feel that with Colette there is only so far you can go with the line that "times were different then." After all, she was able to be freethinking and break with convention in so many areas of her life (i.e., the ones that suited her) that it seems fair to hold her to account in other areas too. And her track record is not great.

All the same, I am a huge fan of Colette's colorful life and legacy. She was an extremely unusual figure and a free spirit. She married Willy at the age of twenty and by her late twenties was writing novels under his tutelage. It is notable that she is frequently referred to in biographical information as "a woman of letters" (not something you would bother calling Sagan or Duras). This is because Colette came from that age, certainly, but it's also because it's slightly more difficult to judge her literary output: she is representative of an era and has not really created a piece of work like *L'Étranger* or *Bonjour Tristesse* that stands on its own outside of that era.

Judith Thurman's biography is one of the most entertaining things you can read about Colette. Especially enjoyable are her photo captions: "A rare photograph of the young marquise de Morny [Missy] dressed (sort of) as a woman." Whatever claims can be made for or against Colette as a literary figure, she's important because she stands for a lot of the reasons many of us are in love with Frenchness: she's glamorous and sexy and fashionable (and even bears a passing resemblance to Coco Chanel); she's theatrical and camp and glorious; she recognizes Frenchness as a brand—even if she didn't voice this, it's obvious from her work—and she isn't afraid to package that up and sell it back to us. In some instances this was even literal, right from the Claudine era, when Claudine outfits, perfume, and makeup were marketed as merchandise.

Certainly, out of all the writers here—and certainly out of the celebrated female French writers—she is a match for the most prolific. And she attained a great degree of success. However, I have to be honest and say that I think her work has probably aged worse than many of the writers here, not in terms of her legacy (which only seems to increase in importance) but in terms of whether you'd actually recommend that anyone read any of her books. Maybe I'm being unfair, seeing as Simone de Beauvoir wrote that Colette "wrote pornographic novels and then good novels." One of the weird things about Colette's work is that she continues to write the same story over and over. This isn't surprising, as this is basically what Willy did for his career, so it was the model for successful publishing that she had seen from early on. (And it worked during her lifetime, so why not?)

Colette is an important writer but not one whose work has stood the test of time. The impact of her life—and her career as a prominent female writer during a period when there were very few—is perhaps more significant than any individual work. Her legacy is about the sweep of her life, the people she influenced, and the circles she moved in. If you compare her with a writer like Balzac, their output word for word is not dissimilar. And yet her legacy is not on the same level. I write this as a feminist who would rather see female writers judged honestly and fairly rather than evaluated as something that they never were. Perhaps, if we are going to be radical about it, it's fair to suggest that her achievement during her own lifetime was greater than anyone else's here. She had the odds stacked against her as a woman in a way that Sagan did not. She came originally from the wrong place, the wrong background, the wrong stock. She had no ambitions to be a writer or an artist. And yet she achieved things that eluded many of the great male writers in this book: fame and wealth, a packed and fulfilled personal life. And a safe exploration of her sexuality that did not result in any syphilis. I think for such a prolific writer this is a huge achievement, and she should be applauded for it.

Many aspects of Colette's life were what my grandmother would call "ahead of her time." She cut her hair short and wore trousers before most women considered this normal. The longest relationship in her life was with Missy, the Marquise de Morny. In the 2018 film, Missy is referred to using the pronoun "he," but in real life there is little evidence that Missy thought of herself as a trans man or that she underwent—as some accounts claimed—some kind of surgery in order to change gender. Whatever the truth of her life, her relationship with Colette was both scandalous and groundbreaking. Certainly, Colette's life was constrained in many ways, but the hallmark of her identity was that she pushed against it. Later on, she had relationships with men considerably younger than her and wrote about this dynamic extensively in her work.

After she split up with Willy, she married Henry de Jouvenel, a newspaper editor. This marriage ended after twelve years, partly because Colette had taken up with her sixteen-year-old stepson. (And you thought Willy was creepy.) I think as time goes by, Colette is likely to be regarded as even more important, thanks to the mythology surrounding her early career: the symbolism of her husband locking her in a room in order to force her to write is very powerful, coupled with the fact that he then published the results under his own name, attempting to airbrush her out of history. She, of course, was having none of that.

If Colette's writing became predictable and reflective of a more conservative era, her life toward the end of her marriage to Willy and afterward was the complete opposite. In 1907, she and Missy appeared onstage in Rêve d'Egypte in a romantic clinch, with Missy dressed as a male archeologist. It's not clear what was more shocking to the audience: the cross-dressing or two women kissing.

Their relationship was complicated: Colette maintained some connections to Willy. Missy often complained that she may have "won," but she was still second best. All the same, Colette wore a necklace engraved with the words "I belong to Missy." The two of them, Missy and Colette, ruled the gossip columns of the time, often with Missy getting more column inches than Colette.

In their biography of her extraordinary life, Claude Francis and Fernande Gontier report that every self-respecting French girl wanted to dress like Missy: "What do young girls dream of?" wrote Le Courrier Français. "Of looking like a certain Marquise." Missy launched a fashion for chartreuse cocktails ("la marquise"). She was extremely wealthy and invested in magazines and cinema. Missy was certainly aristocracy of sorts, with the most ridiculous family tree imaginable: a descendant of Louis XV, granddaughter of Napoléon III's niece Hortense. But even that was not enough for the Missy myth: it was also said that she was Sarah Bernhardt's secret half sister and/or the granddaughter of Tsar Nicholas I. Missy was a key piece of the Colette puzzle. She was the person Colette perhaps wished she could be: financially independent (because she was born into the aristocracy) and entirely free.

In a sense, perhaps, Colette did get the freedom that she wanted: she lived to the age of eighty-one. She died in 1954, having published more novels in the post-war period and having lived out the last decade of her life as the most famous living author in France. She was the first female writer to be given a state funeral.

That's a major achievement. Plus, there's something telling about the lesson in *Gigi*. It's a hopelessly outdated story that belongs in the nineteenth century rather than in the time when Colette was writing it. But something about this story has survived into our era in the form of movies like *Clueless* and *Legally Blonde*. We pretend that we're over these portrayals of women who dream of being rescued or who are looking for a Prince Charming. But still they persist. *Gigi* is a slightly messier Cinderella story: the girl is transformed and, with her, the man who loves her. It's not deep, and it's clearly a fairy tale. But it's one with a message worth remembering: we can't all be born with agency and choices. Gigi has to make the best of what she's got and won't allow herself to be shamed for it. Colette is a frothy glass of vintage Champagne who serves as a useful reminder of how fast things can change—and how colorful are the lives of those who are involved in changing them. We should all drink to that.

4. No one can be truly happy while others suffer: *Les Misérables* by Victor Hugo

(Or: There are times when you need to write in your underpants)

BY THE TIME I had been learning French for a few years, I could cope with a lot of conversations and understand almost everything I needed to. One of the proudest moments of my entire life came when I managed to make an excellent joke in French, almost by mistake. I was watching television with my pen pal's family. The Pet Shop Boys were performing live on a Saturday night chat show. At the time their stage act consisted of Neil Tennant singing passionately at the front and Chris Lowe playing the keyboards glumly in the back. Actually, I don't know why I'm saying "at the time." This is and always has been their stage act. When the keyboard player's face flashed up on screen, my French pen pal's father said, *"Pourquoi ne sourit-il jamais?"* ("Why does he never smile?") Instinctively, without thinking, I replied, *"Peut-être qu'il n'a pas de dents."* ("Maybe he has no teeth.") The entire family turned round to stare at me, amazed, and cracked up. I had crossed over. It felt good.

Still, though, there were things that I didn't understand or that took me by surprise. Not long after this surprising dental humor triumph, I was shopping on my own in a jewelry store in Angers, where my host family lived, and picked up a pair of giant neon green flower earrings. They were the sort of thing most people would hate: loud, garish, completely pointless. I had to have them. I took them to the cashier, slightly embarrassed at my own lack of taste. *"Ils sont un peu fous . . ."* ("They are a bit crazy . . ."), I said apologetically. The woman behind the counter smiled at me and shrugged. *"Bof. Quelquefois il faut craquer."* For a moment, I frowned and looked confused. I didn't know this verb *"craquer."* But I could guess at it. What a genius expression! "Oh well, sometimes you just have to lose your head." Or: "Hey, sometimes you've got to crack." *Quelquefois il faut craquer.* It's a fantastic justification for allowing yourself to do something selfish or ill-advised. It's definitely part of the recipe for happiness.

But it's only one part of the recipe. Sagan, Proust, and Colette were happy to lose their heads over plenty of things: summertime, madeleines, Missy. But Victor Hugo would argue that this is only a partial joy. Is it even real happiness if it's just self-indulgence? Where Colette's work is a celebration of hedonism, fueled by the excesses and new permissiveness of the early twentieth century, the writing of Victor Hugo, only a few decades earlier, is a paean to altruism. Other writers might want to explore pleasure and redefine fun. Hugo is here to remind us that our fun is frequently paid for by someone else's suffering. What's the happiness lesson here? It's the fate of Jean Valjean. He might have a hard life. But he lived it right. And, most important, he found joy through self-sacrifice. Here's someone who would definitely have kept his head and put the neon green earrings back. *Il n'aurait pas craqué.* (He would not have cracked. Sorry, I said I wouldn't say things in French and now I have. *Je m'excuse.*)

I resisted reading Victor Hugo for a long time. First, because I was irritated by the colossal reputation of the musical and film versions of *Les Misérables*. I had, I thought, missed the party because I'd accessed the story so many times through the songs that I didn't think I'd be able to get much from the original book. Second, I thought he would make me . . . yes, miserable. Well, it's in the title, isn't it? Also, aside from seeing signs for Place Victor Hugo in Paris, he wasn't someone whose work felt alive for me in the sense that no one I knew in France ever mentioned him. As a teenager I listened to a lot of French pop music. The singers Mylène Farmer quoted Baudelaire and Patricia Kaas mentioned Arthur Rimbaud. But no one seemed that interested in Victor Hugo.

I realized much later that this was possibly because he had been the giant of them all for so long that perhaps everyone got fed up with him. Hugo was known as the greatest French writer within his lifetime and for decades afterward. He was also known to be a godlike figure, a bit like a real-life superhero. Hugo developed the reputation literally of a superhuman being. Although instead of X-ray vision, which might have been useful, he supposedly had legendary hearing and, when he was in the countryside, was able to tell the difference between an ant and a mole beneath the ground. This seems an incredibly pointless life skill but impressive nonetheless. His biographer Graham Robb writes: "He could eat half an ox at a single sitting, fast for three days and work non-stop for a week." Now we're talking. That's useful. The hair on his face was said to grow so fast that he blunted the blade of a razor three times faster than any other man. Basically if you are looking for the writer who most closely resembles Drax from *Guardians of the Galaxy*, then that person would be Victor Hugo, with the addition of a Santa Claus beard. Victor Hugo also has the best claim to the title of Most Stereotypical

French Author, not a title anyone would ever like to hold. His life and tastes are easily parodied and exaggerated. And he holds a fascination even for those uninterested in French literature because he's the author of a story that has touched so many lives in the unlikely form of a musical.

I often wonder what would have happened if anyone tried to make a musical of *À La Recherche du Temps Perdu*. I just don't think it could end up on the same level as *Les Misérables* in terms of either plot or empathy, and it would have to be about three days long. Also, in terms of the surrounding PR, Hugo's life and reputation lend themselves to a mainstream retelling in a way that Proust's never could. When the BBC television adaptation of *Les Misérables* (not a musical, much to some people's delight) aired, I was thrilled to read an account of Victor Hugo in the British tabloid newspaper the *Sun*. This is not a place you would usually expect to read about Victor Hugo. But it turned out he was ripe for treatment in those pages, where the great author was painted as having "a voracious sexual appetite, with a taste for whores." The paper added, "The randy Frenchman was a foot fetishist, a voyeur and even seduced the girlfriend of his own son." This report excitedly went on to say that Hugo boasted of having sex nine times on his wedding night. And that he wrote *The Hunchback of Notre-Dame* virtually naked ("wearing a scratchy woolen body stocking") in order to cool his sexual urges. I had never thought of a woolen body stocking as a form of a cold shower before. But I suppose I may have led a sheltered life. The opposite of Victor Hugo, clearly.

So you get the picture. There's a lot going on with Victor Hugo. It makes sense that over 130 years after his death, Hugo is still surrounded by larger-than-life myths. Of all the authors featured here, he was perhaps the one who had the biggest success in his lifetime. This was despite the fact that when *Les Misérables* first came out, it was not favorably received. Flaubert said that as a piece of work it was "infantile" and that it represented the end of Victor Hugo's career. Initially few critics were impressed with Hugo's attempt to combine visionary politics and storytelling. Baudelaire declared that this was the kind of propaganda that didn't belong in art and that the book was "inept."

At the same time, though, it represented one of the greatest literary coups in history and was to become the crowning glory of Hugo's life. In *The Novel of the Century: The Extraordinary Adventure of* Les Misérables, David Bellos estimates that the deal Hugo struck for *Les Misérables* was worth £3 million in today's money. That is a lot of pressure. But it didn't seem to bother Victor Hugo too much. He was a man who took a lot of things in stride. And despite criticisms from some of his contemporaries, the book went on to become a huge bestseller, echoing the reception of bestsellers even today. It was a story that captured the Zeitgeist and did something many novels aspire to do but few actually achieve: combine the emotional brilliance of a piece of art with a passionate political message about the necessity of eradicating poverty.

In his lifetime and for some time afterward, Victor Hugo was both a celebrity author and a celebrity Frenchman, though he was not "people" in the sense of that word I love. He was a genuinely admirable figure who did not seek fame for its own sake. Arguably in later years his reputation became eclipsed by Proust, who I think more readers would be more likely to name now as the most famous French author, largely and almost exclusively because of the madeleines.

Nonetheless, despite this cake-based usurping of his legacy, Hugo possesses, perhaps, something even greater than Proust: a novel so well-known that it has eclipsed its author.

It's slightly embarrassing for us in the modern era that we've boiled Hugo's legacy down to a piece of musical theatre. And I say that as someone who loves musical theatre. I absolutely don't mean this in a snobby way, as I adore all versions of Les Mis: the stage version, the film version, the BBC TV adaptation. Literary purists hate the fact that there are musical theatre fans who can sing "I Dreamed a Dream" with exactly the same intonation as Anne Hathaway but who have not read a word of the novel and probably never will. I don't think this is a bad thing. Storytelling is storytelling, and Hugo more than anyone appreciated having a platform, and the success of that musical has given his story an extraordinary platform. It matters less how you come to a piece of art than what you take away from it.

Hugo originally started working on Les Misérables under the title Jean Tréjean, later Les Misères. It is surprisingly difficult to piece together the circumstances in which Victor Hugo wrote the novel. Hugo appears to have gathered ideas for Les Misérables over several decades and worked on the novel on and off over a period of around twenty years. The period described in the novel is 1815 to 1832, but Hugo wrote it in the 1850s, and Les Misérables was not published until 1862. Hugo most likely conceived the idea for Les Misérables in the early 1840s, although some trace the idea back to the late 1820s, when his focus began to switch toward the political. We do know that in 1839 he visited a prison in Toulon and wrote the name JEAN TREJEAN in capital letters in his notes. In 1831, The Hunchback of Notre-Dame had been a commercial success, and he began to consider a career in politics. Without him consciously thinking this, *Les Misérables* was a way of joining up the two halves of his interests. He started writing in 1845, but events overtook him with the Revolution of 1848, and he was forced to devote himself to politics. Hugo was known for his excellent public speaking in the political chamber, although he said that he found speaking "as exhausting as three ejaculations," which surely has to count as the nineteenth-century definition of too much information.

Ejaculations aside, where they should be, there is a three-part element to the narrative in *Les Misérables*: Jean Valjean represents the harm that poverty, both material and spiritual, can do to a man; Fantine illustrates what happens to a woman when she is forced to sell herself to eat; and Cosette shows the danger of raising a child in darkness. The novelist Adam Thirlwell calls this almost-Biblical idea "the triad of the needy." Hugo was explicit about this "man, woman, child" aspect of the story and referenced it in an oft-used quote that expressed his desire for *Les Misérables* to be seen as a universal story about humanity (and not one about a uniquely French experience): "Wherever men go in ignorance or despair, wherever women sell themselves for bread, wherever children lack a book to learn from or a warm hearth, *Les Misérables* knocks at the door and says, 'Open up, I am here for you.'" This strikes me as beautiful but also melodramatic. Yes, Victor Hugo was a total and utter ham, and you've got to love him for it.

Hugo's stated aims were extraordinarily modern and later to become a commonplace idea: that politics is history and shapes history; that history is not just about great events and key facts and figures, it is also about the experience of so-called ordinary people. This was the kind of "from the ground up" historical theory that became prevalent in the twentieth century, when historians started digging around for evidence of how life was really lived and why people thought the way that they did, rather than the sort of chronological, aristocratic history that focuses on the lives of kings and queens. Hugo and *Les Misérables* played a significant role in this way of thinking.

What is the reading experience of *Les Misérables*, though? Of all the books mentioned here, it is the one that people will annoy you the most by saying, "Oh, you really must read the original novel." As you will have guessed, I have no truck with people who refer to "the original novel," using that precise phraseology, as if to imply that they are the only people in the world who realize that it was a novel first. This kind of thinking has been prevalent for a long time. But I think it's starting to break down, especially now that many people are happy to say that they would much rather "hear" a novel as an audio book, that they would rather listen to podcasts than digest words through their eyes, and now that many writers are devoting themselves to creating stories in different media other than novels—writing television screenplays, for example. I often think about Victor Hugo in this context. Wouldn't he have loved for *Les Misérables* to have the impact of a podcast like *Serial*, which is, in its own way, trying to do what he was trying to do: reexamine how we process story, ask what justice is, and put our biases under the microscope? I don't think Victor Hugo would be annoyed by the success of *Les Misérables* the musical, and he wouldn't even have stressed out that much about Russell Crowe's singing. In the same way I don't think Hugo would have insisted on the reading of the novel to access the "true meaning."

So should you read the novel? Obviously I think you should. But only if it will bring you pleasure and insight. It is handily arranged in 365 chapters, so in theory you could read a chapter a day for a year and feel very virtuous about yourself. Be warned, though, that Les Misérables is packed full of digressions, philosophical essays, and treatises on morality and politics, many of which Hugo signposts, as if to say, "It's OK, you don't have to read this bit." At its heart, though—and almost certainly at the heart of its enduring appeal as a story—it is the tale of a hero, one of the most extraordinary everyman characters in global literature, Jean Valjean. Although I would argue that there are in fact two main characters in Les Misérables, of equal weight: Jean Valjean and the Coincidence.

Indeed, one of the only ways to understand Les Misérables, which is so full of overlapping destinies and improbable coincidences as to make your eyes swivel, is to imagine that France is a country populated by about forty-three people. Then it makes total sense. (In fact the population in 1850 was about thirty-six million.) Hugo's great trick with this novel is to make all this seem completely normal. On the surface, it's about the intertwined fates of Jean Valjean, a reformed convict, and Fantine, a young woman who has had her heart (and life) broken by a young playboy and has been left destitute and pregnant. When Jean Valjean reestablishes himself in civilian life as a factory owner and mayor under the alias Monsieur Madeleine, Fantine ends up in his employ, having left Cosette, her baby, to be looked after by the Thénardiers family.

When it comes to light that Fantine has an illegitimate child, she is thrown out of the factory and is forced into prostitution in order to keep up her payments to the Thénardiers. She attacks a man on the street for harassing her and comes to the attention of the local police inspector, Javert, who was an adjutant guard (no, I don't know what this is either) at the prison where Jean Valjean did his time. Javert has had his suspicions about "Mayor Madeleine" for a while, especially when he witnessed the mayor rescue a man trapped under a heavy cart. Javert has never witnessed this kind of brute strength in a man before—except in a prisoner he once knew. Meanwhile, the rescued man, named Fauchelevent, disappears to be a gardener at a convent in Paris, as you do when you've just been rescued from the jaws of death underneath a cart.

As for Javert and his appalling inability to recognize people he already knows . . . I always tend to think at this point that Javert either must have had terrible eyesight or face blindness. Jean Valjean, with or without a convict beard, was a pretty distinctive character. I'm not sure you would spend so long thinking, "Hmm, I'm sure that face is familiar . . ." Yes! It's someone you knew in prison for nineteen years! Hugo spends a long time describing Javert's face (one and a half pages at one point), likening him to a wild beast, a tiger, and a mastiff. But perhaps the clue lies here: "You could not see his forehead, which disappeared under his hat. You could not see his eyes that lurked beneath his eyebrows." Clearly Javert had such a big hat and so much eyebrow hair that he can barely see anything at all.

Much to Javert's consternation, he discovers that a man going by the name Jean Valjean (I know, crazy, right?) is on trial and has been sentenced to death. "Monsieur Madeleine" cannot let this happen. Side note: my favorite sentence in the entire novel, aside from the bits where Hugo says "It is one of the narrator's privileges" when he time-travels randomly from one storyline to another, is this, from part 1, book 7, chapter 3:

"The reader has no doubt guessed that Monsieur Madeleine is none other than Jean Valjean." For it is none other than he! Assuring Fantine that he will pay off the Thénardiers and return soon with Cosette, "Monsieur Madeleine" heads off to hand himself in and stop the trial of Non-Jean-Valjean. The court agrees that Real-Jean-Valjean may return home, where he will be officially arrested by Javert. When he does, Javert is with Fantine, ready and waiting for him. Fantine sees her hero humiliated, Javert vindicated. She promptly drops dead from shock, without having seen her child for a final time.

Here we come to the two intertwined fates that really matter in this novel, in my view: not Jean Valjean and Fantine—whose daughter, Cosette, effectively becomes Jean Valjean's own child—but Valjean and Javert. These two circle each other throughout, cat-and-mouse style. Hugo may have had the idea that he's representing *"les misérables"* through the lives of Valjean and Fantine, but in reality the character who is most symbolic is always Javert. He is the self-righteous fool who cannot see that there are two sides to every story and that it is possible to be legally right but morally wrong. He is the opposite of revolution, compassion, and progress.

Jean Valjean, having escaped from prison, rescues Cosette from the Thénardiers family, after many shenanigans. They settle in Paris but are eventually tracked down by Javert. Again, this is where it helps to believe that there are only a few dozen people in Paris. Otherwise, in a city of millions and with no internet or facial recognition software, is it even possible for a moment that Javert would find Jean Valjean? Thankfully, owing to the coincidence of Almost-Crushed-Under-a-Cart (remember him?) Fauchelevent working in a convent, Jean Valjean and Cosette go and hide there so that Javert can't find them. One fact that has already been well-established in this book is that if you are in trouble, get some religious people to hide you because they are really good at lying convincingly.

Eight years pass. (Don't question this.) There are still hardly any people living in Paris, therefore the paths of many people we have already met are destined to cross. A young student named Marius Pontmercy is clashing with his authoritarian grandfather. Marius wants to find a man mentioned in a letter left to him by his dead father, a colonel. As a young man, the life of Colonel Georges Pontmercy was saved at Waterloo by a man called—guess what?—Thénardiers. From here on Hugo goes completely insane for coincidences. The Thénardiers are also in Paris now. And they happen to be living in the same residence where Cosette and Jean Valjean lived before hiding in the convent. And Marius the student is their next-door neighbor. And Marius has also seen Cosette in the park and fallen in love with her. And—stay with me here—Éponine, the Thénardiers' daughter, has fallen in love with Marius.

Now, I love this novel, so I am trying to not get annoyed here. But it does all get a bit silly, and you have to overlook a lot. (Whenever I am moaning about this book, my husband always gives me a really annoying look and says, "Oh. Is it making you . . . miserable?" And then he laughs for about three hours.) Because this is where it is the turn of both Jean Valjean and Thénardiers to get lavish eyebrow hair in their field of vision. Jean Valjean is now living as "Monsieur Leblanc" and has become a philanthropist who is comfortable enough to be able to help the poor. Guess who needs help? The Thénardiers family, now living under the name Jondrette. "Monsieur Leblanc" visits the "Jondrette" family and—get this—neither of them recognize either other. After only eight years. That is a serious amount of eyebrow hair getting in the way. Yes, "Jondrette" (Thénardiers) has an inkling. But he doesn't realize straightaway. When Thénardiers does cotton on, he decides to attack Jean Valjean, firstly out of revenge for his "taking" Cosette and second because he thinks Jean Valjean is rich and he can steal from him. This plot is conveniently overheard by next-door neighbor Marius, who reports him to . . . Guess who? Javert. Of all the police inspectors in all the districts of Paris . . .

The coincidences pile up as the cat-and-mouse game between Javert and Jean Valjean reaches its conclusion and the revolutionary masses gather at the barricades. Thénardiers kidnaps Valjean and threatens Cosette. Marius gets stressed because he realizes Thénardiers is a crook but is also the man who rescued his father in battle. (In fact Thénardiers was looting his not-actually-dead corpse.) Éponine gets upset because Marius loves Cosette. Jean Valjean rescues nearly dead Marius from the barricade, carries him through a sewer, and still remains unrecognizable to Thénardiers, who just happens to be by the sewer door Jean Valjean comes out of. (And breathe.) Jean Valjean pretends to shoot Javert but releases him, and Javert is so perturbed by this act of clemency that he commits suicide. And just when you think everything is going to work out fine and Marius and Cosette can get married, Thénardiers pops up again. After seeing Valjean in the street (and finally recognizing him as the man from the sewer), Thénardiers has him followed. Thénardiers realizes Jean Valjean is connected to Marius and hopes he can squeeze some money out of Marius by revealing the "truth" about the past. Thénardier's pièce de résistance is that he has a scrap of cloth torn from the coat of the "corpse" Jean Valjean was carrying in the sewer. This is supposed to "prove" that Jean Valjean is a murderer. But all it proves is that Jean Valjean saved Marius's life. But it's too late, because Jean Valjean has already gone to the countryside to die.

At this point I always get confused about why Jean Valjean did not want Marius to know that he saved his life. But basically it's because Jean Valjean didn't want Marius and Cosette to feel indebted to him. Fair enough. Although if I had saved someone's life by carrying them through a sewer, I would want them to feel extremely indebted to me. And I would probably take out an advert in the paper about it so that everyone would know how great I was. But that, my friends, is why I am not Jean Valjean.

It's extraordinary to me how Hugo managed to keep all this in his head and tie up all the loose ends. In fact, considering that you need a sort of family tree of several pages in order to understand the links between all these different characters, it is not surprising that most people over the past 150 years have chosen to imbibe this story via the medium of song. When it was first released, though, readers lapped it up. The book sold out in Paris within three days. It's hard to imagine how ardently people wanted to read this book and what it meant to them. It was banned by the Catholic Church and publicly burned in Spain. Factory workers pooled their resources in order to buy a single copy. The critics hated it and regarded it as a book for people who couldn't read. But Hugo had achieved his aim: he had wanted people to understand that this was a profound story about injustice and the need for change, about the things we cannot put up with.

Nonetheless, although Hugo was a successful author, and a celebrated one, he worried that his concerns for the poor would be seen as hypocritical. His biographer Graham Robb regards it as a "guilt offering" to offset the double life that Hugo was leading: "A statistical analysis shows that from 1847 to 1851 he had sex with more women than he wrote poems." And he wrote a lot of poems. But clearly he didn't feel that bad about it, as by the 1870s he was happily playing the part of the Great Writer. And as part of the "salon" atmosphere where people came to pay court to the Great One, ladies not wearing gloves would be kissed from fingertips to elbow. If you were trying to pull a fast one on the old goat and keep your gloves on, he'd stick an exploratory finger underneath the gloves and have a wiggle around.

Hugo was a fascinating mix of social campaigner, feted writer, sex maniac, and egotist. As his fame increased, the Hugo name spawned many eponyms in French, from *Hugotiste* (Hugo fan) and *Hugocrate* (Hugo obsessive) to *Hugolisme* (similarity-to-Hugo), and the verb *"hugolâtrer"* (to idolize Hugo). One of the worst side effects of Hugolatry was experienced by a poet who supposedly died from self-loathing after a house visit where he accidentally smashed a vase belonging to the great writer. The English writer Algernon Charles Swinburne, a man known for writing about lesbianism and cannibalism (crazy guy!), wrote that he dreamed of polishing Hugo's boots every day. To his credit, whenever this boot-polisher came round to stan him in person, Hugo pretended not to understand any English and, later, to be deaf.

When I think of Victor Hugo now, though, I cannot avoid thinking of him as a man with bad hair. The few pictures of him in existence show a man with a receding hairline who did everything he could to make up for what he was losing up top by growing it down the sides. Come on, Victor, we know what you're trying to do there. Clearly this was no barrier to his success with the ladies. Juliette Drouet was Hugo's mistress for fifty years and wrote him over twenty thousand letters. I dread to think how many more she would have written if email had existed. I'm amazed they had any time for sex.

He was married to Adèle Foucher for forty-six years, and they had six children together. Both had affairs, and Hugo had multiple liaisons with prostitutes, which was entirely normal for his social status and his profession. It seems a complete miracle that he didn't get syphilis. It's easy to paint a slightly monstrous picture of him thanks to his "secret code" diaries where, among other aberrations, women's breasts were referred to as "Switzerland" (because of milk production).

But there are many redeeming details in his biography, not least his devastated reaction to the drowning of his daughter Léopoldine when she was nineteen. She had just married, and her husband died trying to save her. Many of his most famous poems were inspired by Léopoldine. He might have loved Switzerland, but he also loved his family. One of my favorite pictures of Hugo is with his grandchildren, Jeanne and Georges. He has accepted his receding hairline and looks like a groomed, self-respecting, svelte Father Christmas. He lived with his grandchildren in later life and encouraged them to share his love of gastronomy, which meant urging them to eat the shells of lobsters (he believed they were good for digestion), to chomp on lumps of coal (good for purging impurities), and to shove oranges whole into their mouths (good for impromptu visits to the ER, I would imagine).

Hugo lived to the remarkable old age of eighty-three, enjoying several city-wide celebrations of his life before he died. The crazed Hugolatry of the later years meant that there was a frenzy around Hugo's deathbed as various people attempted to report his last words, which resulted in him having an extremely long stream of reported last words that turned out not to be his last words. It also resulted in a man who claimed to have been Hugo's manservant selling four hundred pairs of "authentic Victor Hugo trousers" at his funeral. Something we'd all wish for, I'm sure. Hugo was to lie in state at the Panthéon, a place he'd previously said he hated because it reminded him of a giant sponge cake. Thousands came to see him lying there and gawp at the souvenirs on sale: wreaths of flowers with his portrait at the center, postcards, and poems. Robb writes that "the whores of Paris had draped their pudenda in black crepe as a mark of respect," but being an owner of pudenda (and a fan of black crepe), I am struggling to picture exactly what this looks like. (They wore black underwear for the night? They put offcuts of cloth over their bits?) The numbers at the funeral the next day were said to be over two million, which is impressive (and telling of the myth surrounding Hugo) but also unlikely, as that was more than the entire population of Paris. For me, the joy of Hugo is the whole larger-than-life business of him, which is brilliantly represented in the character of Jean Valjean: a bear of a man, stronger than an ox, the heart of a lion, a man strong enough to rescue someone from underneath a heavy cart . . . A man who tames his animalistic appetites in favor of compassion and generosity. A man who discovers faith—in himself and in others. "To love another person is to see the face of God," says Hugo, through Jean Valjean.

This is the heart and soul of the message of Les Misérables: your true worth is determined by what you do for others. Without it ever being explicitly stated, it feels as if for

Hugo, personal happiness is intimately linked to having a clear conscience. The book is intricately plotted, and the dilemmas his characters face are often nuanced. This is Hugo's round-about way of demonstrating that these matters are not simple: sometimes Jean Valjean must do what is "wrong" (lie about who he is, for example) in order to do what is "right" (protect Cosette). He can only learn from experience how he really feels about his deeds. Do they allow him to sleep at night? Does he feel at peace with himself? He makes a lot of mistakes before coming to terms with the sort of person he needs to be. And it's confusing for Jean Valjean, because his moral instincts often go against what is expected of him by society.

Similarly Javert appears to do everything by the book. He has a clear conscience because he follows the letter of the law. And yet we know that his cruel, uncompromising behavior is, while lawful, a crime against humanity. What really breaks Javert—and kills him in the end—is his confrontation with a harsh fact: true contentment and peace of mind come not from following external rules and regulations but from an intimate knowledge of your own internal moral compass and what it will and won't tolerate. This is no simple lesson, and it's one Hugo takes his sweet time to impart. He doesn't preach either nor even really take sides. He pays as much attention to Javert and his side of the story as he pays to Jean Valjean. It's clear who we're meant to follow in the end, though: the man who always does the right thing by others even if it involves his own suffering. It's not the easy path. But who ever said happiness was easy? I had better start training for a sewer rescue. I don't want to be found wanting when the moment arrives.

5. Self-deceit is the surest path to misery: *Les Liaisons Dangereuses* by Choderlos de Laclos

(Or: Do not use your naked lover as a writing desk)

IF *LES MISÉRABLES* is about being brutally honest with yourself about right and wrong, then *Les Liaisons Dangereuses* is about confronting yourself with the truth about who you really love. In the guise of a morality tale, this novel is a stark warning about what happens when people lie to themselves about the nature of their emotions. Several lives are ruined simply because two people are too embarrassed to admit that they actually have feelings. The Marquise de Merteuil and the Vicomte de Valmont once had a romantic entanglement that they both played out cynically as if it were a game. Afterward, neither can bring themselves to admit that they are capable of real emotion, and they do everything within their power to humiliate anyone who is silly enough to actually fall in love.

In real life I would have been one of their patsies, easily manipulated and happy to eat up their lies. During the time when I spent several weeks of the year in France as a teenager, I was heavily focused on an achievement the Marquise de Merteuil would have approved of: getting a French boyfriend. The trouble was, this wasn't a game or a pose for me; for a time this was my sincere life's quest. The picture I had in my mind of the ideal Frenchman came straight out of Choderlos de Laclos: a dark, mysterious cad like the Vicomte de Valmont. A heartbreaker, basically. In reality, the French boys I knew were all small and shy and had fairly noticeable body odor. (To be fair, Vicomte de Valmont probably also had the latter.) I attempted to work with what was available, but my efforts were rarely successful. I did once get a boy called Hervé Cheval to take me to the ice rink. I was very excited about the prospect of being called Madame Cheval (Mrs. Horse), and I noted that I already had both a physique and demeanor far better suited to this name than his were. However, thanks to the fact that I was twice his size, clumsy, and overly enthusiastic, I managed to pull him down onto the ice, nearly dislocating his shoulder, like a particularly unerotic version of Johnny Hallyday's dead horse. So that was the end of that.

The most stereotypical view of the French is that all French men and all French women are the sexiest people in the world and that they are the world leaders in having affairs. I am not sure how this plays into the widely held idea that the French are living their best lives, but I can't help feeling that the two are somewhat related. From what I understand, it's one of those stereotypes that exists for a reason: it is grounded in fact. French men (and women) are permanently looking for sex. As long as you are not an English teenager with bad skin, large thighs, and a propensity for saying *"bof"* rather more than is normal. The subtext of *Les Liaisons Dangereuses* is that in order to facilitate these kinds of extramarital relationships, you have to cultivate a sort of emotional coldness. You cannot afford to actually fall in love. And, the book seems to conclude, there is something monumentally sad about this.

I'm willing to buy the argument that the French don't find affairs morally complicated. What I don't understand is why anyone pretends these affairs don't bring misery. When they clearly do. As a lifelong reader of the problem pages of the French editions of *ELLE*, *Marie Claire*, and *Madame Figaro*, as well as someone who has quizzed French girlfriends on this subject, I do think there are certain truisms that mean that there's a view of extramarital sex that is different to the British or American view. In short, in France, it is more commonly assumed that extra-relational activity will happen than that it won't. For confirmation that this is still true in the twenty-first century, even now that certain standards are changing, you only have to watch the French TV series *Dix Pour Cent* (it's on Netflix, retitled *Call My Agent!*). This show is about a group of five colleagues in an agency for actors and celebrities. The agents are always sleeping with each other. And when they are not doing this, they are trying to prevent their clients from having affairs with each other. Or sometimes they facilitate them. It's all very French. Like I say, stereotypes exist for a reason. Do any of them seem happier as a result of all this sex and deceit? No. But would they be even more unhappy trapped in miserable monogamy? Probably. This is the conundrum.

The best representation in literature of this mentality is the world of the dashing and dastardly Vicomte de Valmont: *Les Liaisons Dangereuses*, a gloriously layered, funny, and clever piece of writing whose intent and underlying meanings are still hotly debated. This was a book whose publication in 1782 caused a scandal on a scale similar to the scandal depicted in the book. According to a 2011 article in *Le Monde* published to mark a new edition of *Les Liaisons Dangereuses*, this was the most read novel of the eighteenth century, reprinted sixteen times in the year of publication. It was unclear whether the Choderlos de Laclos meant this novel as a provocative piece of entertainment intended as a celebration of amorality or as a political statement damning the aristocracy for their decadence and cruelty. Is it a celebration of libertinism? Or a vicious critique of it? The author's intentions can never be known. Which I think is rather wonderful, as it means that we get to decide for ourselves. Furthermore, this book is a perfect example of the sort of book that challenges your expectations and your morality over time. There are times when I can read (or watch) *Les Liaisons Dangereuses* and find it hilarious and delicious and clever. And there are times when I can come to it and think that it is a depiction of the absolute worst of humanity, so much so that it makes me want to weep forever.

I came to this novel as many people would have come to it: thanks to Stephen Frears's 1988 film starring Glenn Close (sublime evil), John Malkovich (almost-as-sublime evil), Michelle Pfeiffer (beautiful, corrupted purity), and Keanu Reeves (unlikely but brilliant as the patsy of the piece). If I were ten years younger, then *Cruel Intentions* would probably have been my entry point, the 1999 modern-day update with Reese Witherspoon, Sarah Michelle Gellar, Ryan Phillippe, and Selma Blair. I love this (extravagantly, brilliantly trashy) film, but I'm a bigger fan of Stephen Frears's version because I think *Les Liaisons Dangereuses* works best within its own period. The ironies are more obvious, and the whole thing is so much more subversive when it's set in the eighteenth century. Of course, though, what I care most about this piece of extremely important work is that on the set of this film Michelle Pfeiffer and John Malkovich had an affair in real life. Yes! In real life! So now you have a measure of what sort of person I really am. (*Très* people.)

The author of the novel is an intriguing character. Say what you like about him, but he was no slouch on the name front. Pierre Ambroise François Choderlos de Laclos was born in Amiens in 1741. Not very much is known about his life, other than the details of his military career and the sprinkling of facts that remain from his (not considerable) correspondence. He spent most of his life as a military officer and wrote the novel that made his name during a six-month vacation period. His aim was to write a work that, in his own words, "departed from the ordinary, which made a noise and which would remain on earth after my death." And he certainly succeeded and then some. Within his lifetime he became as notorious as the Marquis de Sade.

In marked contrast to the Marquis de Sade, however, Choderlos de Laclos is usually described as a family man. He married his wife in 1786 and stayed with her until his death. Alarm bells usually start to ring for me whenever I hear the phrase "family man." It is the marital equivalent of a neighbor described as "quiet" or "a bit of a loner." But in the case of Choderlos de Laclos, it seems as if it was actually true, and he was neither a serial killer nor a relentless philanderer like Victor "one prostitute for every poem" Hugo. Also, happily, he is another of these examples of people who have added "de" to the middle of their names to make themselves seem upper class. I know that in theory we should hate these people for being terrible, ridiculous snobs, but in reality I find their actions rather endearing and demonstrative of the gaping hole of need at their pit of their souls. And who doesn't identify with that?

The story told through a series of letters in *Les Liaisons Dangereuses* appears complicated but is actually very simple. The scandalous tale centers around the Marquise de Merteuil, a powerful widow in her thirties. She wants revenge on Gercourt, a former lover who wronged her. She intends to ruin his wedding night by "spoiling" a beautiful young virgin he intends as his bride, Cécile de Volanges, fresh out of the convent. To assist her in corrupting Gercourt's future bride, the Marquise de Merteuil enlists the assistance of the Vicomte de Valmont. The relationship between Merteuil and Valmont is deliberately ambiguous. It is clear that they were once in love but are no longer together. But it is also clear that they still have feelings for each other. Valmont has similar motivations to Merteuil in this game: Gercourt also humiliated him. Merteuil lost Gercourt to a woman known as "L'Intendante." In turn, L'Intendante left the Vicomte de Valmont to be with Gercourt.

Both the Marquise de Merteuil and the Vicomte de Valmont are Machiavellian and cynical, bound together by their fondness for using other people as playthings. (You've got to love them!) Valmont's reward and incentive will be a renewal of his relationship with Marquise de Merteuil. He, though, suggests upping the stakes: it will be easy to corrupt Cécile. Why not add in another challenge? The saintly Madame de Tourvel, a married woman whose flawless morals and religious devotion are known to all. Not only does Valmont want to conquer her, but he wants Madame de Tourvel to beg him to do it. Long before interior monologue was a device used in fiction, Choderlos de Laclos allows us to see inside all the characters' minds by collecting all of their correspondence. We see Cécile writing to the Marquise de Merteuil (who has, naturally, become her confidante, with Cécile's mother's blessing) about how she is falling in love with her music teacher, Danceny (a young man the Marquise will in her turn seduce). We see Cécile's mother writing to Madame de Tourvel to warn her what a horrible man Valmont is. Letters are copied, forged, and intercepted. All the while Valmont and the Marquise de Merteuil continue with their plan, weakening all the other players and bending them to their whims, using flattery, subterfuge, and deception.

Both Valmont and the Marquise de Merteuil lose patience with each other at different moments and threaten to call off the arrangement. Both fear the other is falling in love with the arrangement rather than with the prospect of the end reward. Both are too cowardly, insecure, proud, and dead inside to admit that they really love each other. Instead, they must break everyone around them in order to feel alive. It's the French way, guys! (Actually it's not confined to France. It's symptomatic of being too rich and too idle.) As the letters draw to their climax, the marriage of Cécile is drawing closer, and Valmont seduces (actually: rapes) her himself to speed things along. The Marquise de Merteuil cannot stop herself from corrupting Danceny too. And when Madame de Tourvel finally succumbs to Valmont's charm—with him having genuinely fallen in love with her, but being unable to admit this to himself—he punishes himself by insisting on pushing her away so that he can attempt to win her back again. This destroys her.

With Madame de Tourvel on her deathbed, humiliated, rejected, and having betrayed all the values that were dear to her, Valmont is forced to fight a duel with Danceny, during which the music teacher lands the killer blow. Before he dies, Valmont hands over the correspondence that will seal the fate of the Marquise de Merteuil. Her reputation in high society is destroyed, and she runs away to the countryside, where she contracts smallpox and goes blind in one eye.

Les Liaisons Dangereuses is a wonderful, playful, languid read precisely because of the letters. I also recommend it for improving your French if you're out of practice or you want to try to get through a full novel. I read it when my French wasn't great and found it manageable. Letters are easier to read than fiction, after all, even if they are fictional letters. The use of the epistolary form screams "unreliable narrator," which is what makes Merteuil's and Valmont's letters so particularly fascinating: we know they are lying to the other letter writers, but are they also lying to each other and to themselves? This is not a comparison I ever expected to make, but I was reminded of the discomfort I feel reading Merteuil's letters in particular when I read about the new book by Jeff Kinney, author of the Diary of a Wimpy Kid series. These are hugely popular children's books told in diary format by the "hero," Greg Heffley. According to Greg's (one-sided) account of his life, he's a great kid with an annoying sidekick, Rowley. In a new book, however, Rowley gets to tell his side of the story in his own diary—and it turns out Greg is a bit of a bully and a meanie. Probably anyone reading the Diary of a Wimpy Kid books already understood that on some level. When we read any one account, there is always a story we're not hearing. By the way, if you're thinking of the film version of *Les Liaisons Dangereuses*, Keanu Reeves is Rowley and John Malkovich is Greg, only they don't fight about rotting cheese. (Although arguably syphilis could well play the role that the Cheese Touch plays in *Diary of a Wimpy Kid*. If you touch the moldy old cheese, you will die.)

The untold story is what keeps us company when we're reading *Les Liaisons Dangereuses*. This effect—rather than the supposedly licentious themes—is what I think has kept this novel current for so long. While Merteuil and Valmont advertise themselves as self-consciously and intentionally unreliable narrators, we know that even in their "honesty" about their unreliability, there is another story at work: the part of themselves they do not show to each other, even as they pretend to show each other everything. This is the part that we see in the mirror in the Stephen Frears's film when the Marquise de Merteuil (played by Glenn Close) is removing her makeup. This part is harder to show in an epistolary novel, especially as we can only "see" this through the eyes of the more "boring" characters.

The creepy, clever, wonderful quality of *Les Liaisons Dangereuses* is that we are the equivalent of Rowley in *Diary of a Wimpy Kid*: we are the ones reading between the lines of the letters between Merteuil and Valmont, looking out for their weakness and humanity, all while they are claiming to manipulate the weakness and humanity of others. We know they are nasty bullies who are manipulating the truth. The ultimate perfect trick of this novel is that Choderlos de Laclos makes us complicit with Merteuil and Valmont: it is their story that delights us more than any other in the novel; they are the characters we most identify with, and yet we are shown at the same time that they are despicable and mean and unforgivable. It's a reminder of a Baudelaire quote: *"Hypocrite lecteur, mon semblable, mon frère."* ("Reader, you hypocrite, my look-alike, my brother.") We read to learn and to judge, but we know while we are reading that we are quicker to judge others than to judge ourselves. And that is what makes us hypocrites.

The 1988 film is a superb rendering of this idea of hypocrisy. This is a film about vanity—and the cost of that. It's a form of vanity that includes pretense: pretending to others that your feelings are not what they really are, pretending that you don't feel as deeply as you do. It opens with Glenn Close checking her reflection in the mirror. The first full four minutes of the film are taking up with dressing rituals, complete with the Marquise de Merteuil being sewn into her dress around her cleavage and Valmont holding a mask up to his face as his servants powder his hair. The message is clear: these people are not what they seem; they are playing roles in a pantomime. There's an attempt in the film to examine the Marquise de Merteuil's feminist credentials, which have also been touched on in academic critiques. You could see her as an extraordinarily forward-thinking role model: she refuses to be controlled by men and has found a way to operate in a universe that is supposed to keep women down. Valmont's aunt, a friend to Madame de Tourvel, sums up women's role in this society: "Men enjoy the happiness they feel. We can only enjoy the happiness we give. They are not capable of devoting themselves exclusively to one person. So to hope to be made happy by love is a certain cause of grief." The Marquise de Merteuil will not play by the rules set by others. However, in establishing her own rules, she has debased herself to a level that is almost subhuman: she cannot both win and remain a decent human being.

There are a lot of clues in the original text to suggest that Choderlos de Laclos did not mean this purely as an entertaining piece of gossip. In some ways, you could laugh at Madame de Tourvel and how she is "played" by the two schemers, and at her piety, which is, in the end, easily eroded. However, you can also read her as a tragic, beautiful, and noble character, a lamb to the slaughter. It has been pointed out that

Tourvel is an anagram of "True Lov(e)." Merteuil is a sugges-tion of *"mortel"* (fatal—she is a killer). Valmont is supposed to represent the choice between "high" (*mont*—mountain) and "low" (*val*—valley) in life. He can choose to follow his heart and be true to Madame de Tourvel, or he could follow his most base impulses and corrupt himself to please Merteuil. There is something interesting about this theory. Valmont appears at first to be on the same level as Merteuil, but in the end he has been her plaything and he pays the price. She does too, of course, but that was unintentional. Valmont could be seen as the everyman who is choosing between true love (the path of righteousness) and mortality (death). Perhaps it is a more religious text than it seems.

The novelist André Malraux has argued that what is interesting about this novel is that it displays psychological techniques: instead of forcing people to do things, Merteuil and Valmont simply suggest and persuade. They never actu-ally make anyone do anything. They make others complicit in their own downfall. This is true also of the relationship between Merteuil and Valmont: she doesn't make him give up Madame de Tourvel; she simply puts the idea in his mind and makes it appear as if he thought of it. In a strange way, the novel exerts the same influence on the reader: we are just captivated by the evil plan and we go along with it.

I must admit a terrible thing about this book, which I hope is true for other readers too and does not mark me out as a weirdo. I love this book and have torn through it many times. However, I always read it the same way: racing ahead to the Merteuil and Valmont letters. They are the (black) heart and soul of this book.

As *Le Monde* noted in its celebration of the latest edition of the novel, Merteuil and Valmont often seem less interested in what they are doing than completely in love with their own intelligence and their schemes. It is their self-awareness that makes this novel entirely strange and original. And it is the character of the Marquise de Merteuil who is really quite extraordinary. She is one of the most feminist literary depictions of a woman before the twentieth century, venal and immoral, far more intelligent than her most cunning adversary and capable, as she says herself, of being a thousand times worse than the worst man: *"Qu'avez-vous donc fait, que je n'aie surpassé mille fois?"* "What have you ever done that I haven't surpassed a thousand times?"

For me, though, one of the great pleasures of *Les Liaisons Dangereuses* is the use of suspense. One of the hallmarks of comedy of any kind is the setup and the rug-pull: setting something up in a certain way and then pulling the rug away to reveal something completely different. The first letter sets the tone perfectly here. Cécile, recently released from a convent, is writing to her friend Sophie. She begins the letter by saying that she is convinced she is to be introduced to her future husband. Why else would her mother have taken her out of the convent? Then she learns that a man has arrived at the house, is called to see her mother, and breaks off from her letter . . . When she returns to the letter, she reveals what happened. A man was introduced to her, and she almost fainted with excitement and horror. Then she promptly learned that he was a shoemaker who had come to measure her foot.

This is a brilliant setup for the beginning of this novel in which suspense, intimacy, and intakes of breath about what might be about to happen next carry all the plot. It's amusing to note that this book was banned in France for obscenity when most of it is taken up with describing things exactly like this meeting with the shoemaker: something exciting and passionate and romantic could be about to happen . . . but invariably is something quite different. This is one of the delights of the two main "evil" characters, Marquise de Merteuil and Vicomte de Valmont: their understanding of the importance of anticipation. What actually happens in life (and in love) is less important (and less joyful) than the waiting and the longing.

The role of happiness is fascinating in this novel. The experience of reading it is an intensely pleasurable and joyful one, until you suddenly realize that it has a horrific aftertaste. This is Choderlos de Laclos's great talent: he makes you complicit in the whole affair. You enjoyed it in the same way that the Marquise de Merteuil and Valmont enjoyed it at first. You, the reader, become an accessory to their crimes. This is a happiness of sorts, but a warped one. It is very striking in this novel how often the Marquise and Vicomte (the "corrupt" characters) speak of happiness. More so than the other characters. They speak of it in an arch, cynical way and usually only in relation to others or in relation to themselves at another point in time. Happiness is something for other people, and it is a temporary, illusory state that is not to be trusted. The Marquise writes of her current lover—"the Chevalier" (Danceny)—as experiencing "perfect happiness" in being loved by her. But she clearly doesn't care about him. The whole thing is a game to her. And she is laughing at his happiness. (Which would be utterly destroyed if he were to know that she is mocking him and playing him for a fool.) "Happiness" is a pose to be enjoyed only in quotation marks, like being sewn into a dress or putting powder over one's wig. "Look at me: I'm 'happy.'"

The ultimate conflict in Choderlos de Laclos's novel is between the closed, sentimental morality of the "pure" (but boring, pious, and self-deceiving) characters and the libertine, open, immoral, but authentic behavior of Merteuil and Valmont. Who is really free? Who is really happy? Who is living the better life? Neither set of characters, really. But the problem is, if you had to choose, you would probably choose to be the terrible people because they are much more exciting and glamorous. This is what makes this an exceptionally subversive work. Choderlos de Laclos's precise political aims are not clear, or at least we do not have full proof of them. But they seem pretty obvious to me. This is a novel about hedonism and moral corruption among the aristocracy. The characters of Merteuil and Valmont are unnecessarily cruel, relentlessly narcissistic and self-regarding, as well as deceitful and manipulative. They are delightful fictional creations. But they really aren't the people you would want running your country. On the other hand, critics over the years have argued that Choderlos de Laclos was part of the establishment himself. He had the patronage of Louis Philippe II, Duke of Orléans, and Marie Antoinette herself was said to be a fan of the novel. I think he wants to have it both ways: he wants to show the reader that we're all hypocrites, judging the Marquise de Merteuil and Valmont for their corruption, while not-so-secretly wanting to be like them. They—the aristocrats—are morally bankrupt. But, Choderlos de Laclos seems to say with a wink, we're all a bit morally bankrupt.

Despite the novel's ambiguity, I do think Choderlos de Laclos makes it clear by the end that the Marquise de Merteuil and the Vicomte de Valmont are desperately sad creatures who were utterly deluded in their perception of reality. They behaved as if they could see everything so much clearer than everyone else. And yet they missed the one thing that anyone can plainly see: they behave as they do in order to protect themselves from the pain of true love. The author is warning us not to be deceived by cynicism. It may seem like the most sensible, mature, and pragmatic choice. But it means that you miss out on life's true joys. Without vulnerability there is no real trust and no real intimacy. By holding themselves at one remove and behaving like puppet masters, the two Machiavellian antiheroes end up living life as if they are looking at a stage, not participating in it. Better to have felt something real and be humiliated than never feel anything and die numb and regretful.

The ultimate trick of this book, though, is to fool us, the readers, into wanting to be like these two seductive losers. This reminds me of the myth of Frenchness and how it represents an "escape" into a supposedly less repressed, more exciting world. This is very much a myth in many respects, as the French are extremely repressed and conservative, even in the way that they pursue affairs. But we want to be Merteuil and Valmont in the same way that we want to be French: glossier, more sophisticated, more daring, more cultured versions of ourselves. And yet we know that the reality is more complicated—and that, in any case, you cannot be something that you are not.

There are glimpses of the "real" from the Marquise de Merteuil. She says to Valmont that there was a time when they truly loved each other and were happy together. But she cannot risk that again: her emotions have to be held at a remove and switched on and off, as part of the game they are playing. In many ways Merteuil is the character who most closely resembles the author himself. When she writes to Cécile, she says that the most important thing you must do when writing a letter is to remember that you are not writing for yourself, you are writing for the recipient. *"Vous devez donc moins chercher à lui dire ce que vous pensez, que ce qui lui plaît davantage."* ("Seek less to tell him what you think but rather tell him what he wants to hear.") This is what the Marquise de Merteuil does with her letters. But it is also what Choderlos de Laclos does with his novel: he creates the deliciously evil characters we will want to follow. And in doing so, he reveals our own self-deceit.

This is a novel not so much about happiness as about the corruption and commodification of happiness. Valmont wants what he wants. But he only wants it so that he can prove that he really wants nothing and cares about nothing. (If Françoise Sagan is the Queen of *Bof*, he is the King.) The truth is obvious, though: he is hiding his true feelings because he is scared of them. The truth is that he is really in love with Madame de Tourvel ("True love"). He doesn't want to win her for a bet. He really wants to be with her, but he cannot bear the strength of his feelings nor the possibility of rejection. One critic described Valmont's reaction to Madame de Tourvel as "self-forgetful happiness," and this is exactly what he cannot bear to face: the idea that he might have an emotion that he cannot control, which makes him forget himself. This is why perversely, at the end of their relationship, he claims he must leave her for reasons "beyond his control." In fact, the element that he cannot really control is that he has actually fallen in love with her. Valmont is an extraordinary, layered, and brilliant character: despicable, charming, hideous, broken. When the actor Jared Harris played the role onstage, he said that you couldn't play the character without experiencing "some level of disgust with yourself."

Merteuil is operating using a similar form of self-deception. She is the model of self-control: a woman who has studied the behavior of men carefully to see how she can best extract the freedoms that they have for herself while also studying what is expected of women so that she can be seen to pretend to behave like that. If she masters this, she can behave as she likes and she won't be censured or castigated. There is something deeply tragic and calculating about her existence. There is something almost robotic, inhuman about her, rather like the Replicants in *Blade Runner*: she has studied human behavior impeccably but almost so well that she has lost her humanity. For example, she enjoys sex with her husband and experiences pleasure, but she learns to camouflage her true reaction so that her husband will assume that she is a woman who doesn't enjoy sex (that she is "frigid") and therefore won't suspect her of having affairs. Ultimately she gets so caught up in her own lies that she lies to herself about how she really feels about Valmont.

The lesson in happiness in *Les Liaisons Dangereuses* is a simple but profound one: happiness is real, not a pose. If you pretend to be something you're not—and especially if you feign emotions you don't have—sooner or later you will be found out. *Les Misérables* is a demonstration of how meaningless happiness is in the face of the suffering of others. *Les Liaisons Dangereuses* takes this a step further. It's about one of the worst things any human being can do: actively and intentionally destroy the happiness of others. The one pleasure the Marquise de Merteuil and Valmont take is in dismantling any happy moment that others might be experiencing. Choderlos de Laclos shows us what he really thinks of this by giving them their comeuppance. This is a novel that leaves you feeling unsettled and unsure as to how exactly you've been manipulated. It also leaves you with a feeling that if you have had a rather pedestrian life with few amorous intrigues, no duels, and no syphilis, and you have not ended up marrying someone much shorter than you whose surname is Horse, then very possibly you have had a very lucky escape.

6. Do not judge your own happiness—just let it be: *L'Amant* by Marguerite Duras

(Or: Avoid excessive alcohol consumption)

THE DISCOVERY OF Marguerite Duras's *L'Amant* came at an important time for me. I was studying French in my final year at school and planning to go to university. I was trying to work out what I would do with my life and how to handle my feelings of "foreignness" (real or imagined or entirely fantastical). I was feeling increasingly alienated from my home environment and desperate to belong somewhere, ideally to another culture. I realize now that this had far more to do with the simple fact that I was a teenager—because everyone feels like this at that age—than anything to do with my surroundings. But at the time—also, typically for a teenager—I thought it was just me. When I picked up this short, perfectly formed novel about a young girl who wants to get away but is also frightened about what that means, I felt like it was written specifically for me. Which is, of course, what all the great classics make us feel, especially if they come into our lives at just the right time.

As with *Les Liaisons Dangereuses*, there's a sexual thread running through this book that was definitely not relevant to my life in any way whatsoever. But I think I must have managed to gloss over that and just focus on the bits that did feel familiar to me. I read this initially as a book about a girl who wants to escape her family of origin. When I reread it later, I saw it for what it is: a coming-of-age novel about a young girl who is picked out by an older man as his lover. I definitely wasn't up for this. In the novel the unnamed girl isn't unwilling, but she isn't entirely sure what is going on either. She just knows that she wants to escape her life, and she is curious about sex. The story is darker than *Bonjour Tristesse* (excepting the ending of *Bonjour Tristesse*, which is perhaps one of the blackest—and most sudden—endings in literature). *L'Amant* is mysterious, elegant, exotic.

And it explores a Frenchness left untouched by many of the authors here: colonialism. When I first discovered *L'Amant*, I was very ignorant about France's colonies. I had a pen pal, Patou, short for Patricia, living in Normandy. She was an orphan who had been one of the refugees tragically known as the "Vietnamese boat people," who had fled Vietnam when the war ended in 1975. Around eight hundred thousand people fled Vietnam by sea: France took in at least sixty thousand refugees. (The US took 250,000.) Of course, I didn't understand much of this at the time, as there was no Wikipedia and it wasn't the sort of thing you asked about in letters that you were writing to practice your French. We tended to ask each other, *"As-tu des animaux à la maison?"* ("Do you have any pets?") rather than "What do you think about the response of the international community to the humanitarian crisis in Southeast Asia?" or "Can you tell me about the horrors your family endured as refugees?"

I was less focused on Duras's ability to put a human face on France's relationship with Indochine (Indochina, as Vietnam was then known) than I was on gleaning information about sex and relationships. Coincidentally, soon I was not alone in this. Shortly after I discovered the book, a film version was released in 1992, which featured plenty of nudity and described itself as an "erotic drama." Suddenly many British filmgoers who had previously shown no interest whatsoever in the oeuvre of Marguerite Duras were captivated by her work. The film version of *L'Amant* caused a huge scandal in England, particularly in the sort of newspapers my parents read at the time, which would report at length about how disgusting and immoral a certain woman was, while describing all her disgusting immorality in great detail and printing very large and copious photographs of her in various states of undress.

The novel is about the relationship between a fifteen-year-old girl and a wealthy Chinese man. In the film, the teenage girl was portrayed by a British actress, Jane March, who was seventeen when filming started. She was completely ripped apart in the British press and pilloried as a "the sinner from Pinner" (the London suburb she came from). I can remember being fascinated by all this because the character in the book and the film was roughly the same age as me, and I couldn't imagine being interested in a wealthy Chinese man who was much older than me. Nor could I imagine a wealthy Chinese man of any age being interested in me. Nothing against wealthy Chinese men. I would probably be quite interested in them now, if there are any reading this.

My other interest in the film version of *L'Amant*, incidentally, came from knowing that it was a Claude Berri film. (He was the producer. It was directed by Jean-Jacques Annaud.) I felt intense love and respect for Claude Berri, as he was the man behind the Jean de Florette films (*Jean de Florette* and *Manon des Sources*), which played a huge role in my teenage love of all things French. These films were incredibly successful in the mid 1980s. These novels by Marcel Pagnol were the compulsory texts for my exams when I was seventeen. The films featured the actors Gérard Depardieu, Daniel Auteil, and Emmanuelle Béart, who were at the heart of the French-speaking "people" universe I loved to read about in French gossip magazines, which I considered a brilliant and completely legitimate way to improve my French. I was beginning to become familiar with the names of these people and expect good things from their projects: it gave me a sense of belonging and of being part of something other people around me didn't know about or understand. When you are an adolescent, that is very powerful.

I was not aware of it at the time, but some sort of awareness of cognitive dissonance was starting to muster in my brain. I grew up in a household where you didn't get to find out about Marguerite Duras or Vietnamese refugees, but you were very conscious of the filthy immorality of young women making artistic career choices. I can remember dimly realizing that this was also representative of the difference between Britain and France at this time. They had beautiful arthouse films featuring Catherine Deneuve (who later starred in a fantastic film called *Indochine*). We had *'Allo 'Allo!*, a sitcom about World War II where people spoke in heavy French and German accents and talked about a painting called "the fallen Madonna with ze big boobies." (It was actually very funny but also awful.)

The label "the sinner from Pinner" was important too. It was the moment that I realized that the only British attachment to and engagement with *L'Amant*—or at least the only interpretation I had access to at the time—promoted the idea that it is "wrong" and "naughty" and "sinful" to be foreign and to have emotions and especially to have sex. I could see that there was another way of being. I knew from reading French magazines that the film had been received completely differently over there and was treated with reverence. I had a growing awareness that there were other places on earth where things happened differently. Where people didn't laugh at feelings or at our desperation for happiness. They took these things very seriously indeed.

With all this in mind, when you come to actually read *L'Amant*, the effect is overwhelming. The story behind the film—especially told from the perspective of British tabloids—appears to be tawdry and cheap on the surface. The effect of the novel is anything but. From the opening sentences, this is a raw, affecting, painful, and beautiful story that blurs the boundary between autobiography and fiction. It's clearly a fictionalized memoir, and you can feel the breath of the aged Duras almost wheezing as she writes it, marked by the trauma of the passing years and the havoc alcoholism has wreaked on her life, but brought back to life by the memories of her childhood.

The story behind *L'Amant* is complex and confusing, like many of the tales that Duras liked to weave. There were to be several versions of the story, which turned out to be—I'm deciding—all her own versions of the same autobiographical memories. In a 1991 *New York Times* article about Marguerite Duras, she is described as having "awed and maddened the French public for more than 40 years." She was once interviewed on French television for four hours in the late 1980s, which I think says more about the weirdness of French television producers than it does about Duras, but anyway. Certainly few of her stories added up or made sense, and she gained a reputation as someone who was wrecked by drink.

Drinking formed such an important part of her life and her work that there are even academic papers on the world of Durassian alcohol.

I tend to agree with the academic interviewed in the legendary *New York Times* article who says that Duras should not really be allowed to talk about her work. She should just get on and write. Because the problem is that once she starts talking about it, it makes less sense, not more. When she writes, though, there is something about her use of language that is intoxicating, raw, and poetic. I find it hard to read her without crying. The language is not pretentious or difficult or academic at all. It feels sometimes like someone's unformed diary. In a good way.

There is something heartbreaking and yet also inspiring about the story behind the publication of Marguerite Duras's *L'Amant*. It's the book for which she became best-known and is still most closely associated with. And yet it was the book that she didn't write until she was seventy, having written over thirty books by that point in her life. Of course, she had had a successful career—*Moderato Cantabile*, *Hiroshima Mon Amour* (the screenplay nominated for an Oscar), *Le Ravissement de Lol V. Stein*—but it was really *L'Amant* that sealed her success. It's also arguably her most autobiographical work and perhaps the one that she simply was not ready to write until she was seventy years old.

This novel is very cleverly framed as a long letter or autobiographical passage (perhaps a letter to herself?) interspersed with details from the meeting with "the lover." It's both very simple and very difficult to summarize *L'Amant*. It's a short novel, and very little happens. It is told through the eyes of a young girl (we never find out her name) who is being raised in Sa Dec in the Mekong Delta by her mother, the headmistress of a school. The narrator attends a boarding school in Saigon. Her father has not been around for a long time: he returned to France when he was ill. One day, waiting for the ferry, she notices a man in a car looking at her. There is an attraction there. He is twenty-seven. She is fifteen. Both are clearly lonely. She is looking for an escape route from her family life. He is the heir to a fortune: bored, rich, anxious to please his father. Continuing in a languid, descriptive style, the narrator flits between memories of her family life and memories of her time with the lover. He is kind to her and makes her feel wanted, which she does not feel at home. She is not sure of her feelings toward him and keeps herself at one remove. An air of doom and disappointment hangs over things from the beginning. Inevitably he has to leave her, as his father disapproves of their relationship.

If it reads like an intimate letter to a friend about something that happened fifty years ago, that's because that's exactly what this novel is. Marguerite Duras was born Marguerite Donnadieu in Saigon, Vietnam, then under French control. She lived in Sa Dec between 1928 and 1932. Her parents were both teachers, part of France's outreach program encouraging educators to move to the colonies to teach. Soon after arriving abroad, her father was taken ill and returned to France, where he died. Her mother chose to stay on and raise her daughter and two sons, and the school she ran still exists. Duras was later to write of her mother's disastrous investment around this time: she took on a piece of farmland that was flooded and rendered worthless. It meant that the family grew up in relative poverty. She frequently referred in interviews—confusingly—to her mother as a farmer because her mother was the daughter of farmers. Perhaps this made her mother feel as if she knew what she was doing. But by all accounts, she was deceived about the land. This, combined with the fact that Duras's younger brother was, as she put it, "retarded," marked her childhood irreparably.

Virtually every aspect of her life is worthy of a novel. At the age of seventeen, she left Vietnam for France to study mathematics (as her mother had wanted), changing to political sciences and then law. She joined the Ministry of the Colonies and married the writer Robert Antelme. During the Second World War she worked for the Vichy government in the department that allocated paper supplies to publishers, joined the Communist Party, and became an active member of the French Resistance alongside future president François Mitterrand, who was to become a lifelong friend. Antelme was deported to Buchenwald for his involvement with the Resistance and barely survived the experience. She looked after him upon his return, but they later divorced.

During the war, as if she wasn't busy enough already with all this going on, she wrote her first novel in 1943. She decided to take the pen name Duras after a town in Lot-et-Garonne where her father had a house. For a long time I couldn't figure out why Duras was familiar to me as a place. And then I realized. My parents-in-law used to own a home in France not far from Duras. We would go there to the market because they had an excellent seller of Pineau, a slightly dodgy sherry my grandmother was fond of, and the use of the name frequently occasioned good-natured arguments as to whether it should be pronounced with or without the "s." It is pronounced with the "s." Although if you give me enough Pineau, I will still want to argue about this.

In the 1980s and 1990s, until Duras's death in 1996, French readers were fascinated by her platonic relationship with Yann Andréa, a man thirty years her junior, who became her companion. He had started a correspondence with her when he was a student. They had a sixteen-year friendship that was the subject of intense speculation, partly because it was seen as proof of the egotism and magnetism of writers: the narrative was that she drew him in and wouldn't let him go. *Le Monde* reported that he was not allowed to call her by her first name, nor allowed to use the informal pronoun *"tu."* Yann Andréa played his part, writing letters to anyone who wrote negative reviews of Duras's work, explaining that they had not paid sufficient tribute to her greatness. (God, please, where can I find a companion like this?) I cannot blame the French for being obsessed with this relationship: it was certainly interesting. The 1991 *New York Times* interview is a delightful encounter with both Duras and Andréa: "She wears a plaid skirt and green stockings, he wears leather pants and has a mustache; together they evince images of whimsy, intellect and danger."

L'Amant was written when she knew Yann Andréa, and perhaps it's not outrageous to speculate that—whatever the strangeness of their relationship—his presence brought a peace of mind that meant she was able to face a part of her past she had not been able to tackle before. Or perhaps their age difference meant that she felt ready to meditate on another relationship where there was an age gap—and a power imbalance. *L'Amant* has been read as a novel about coming-of-age and about longing. And it's clearly about eroticism and desire, without ever being seedy or weird. It creates its own moral universe. The narrator writes of the breasts of one of her friends:

"I'd like to eat Hélène Lagonelle's breasts as he [the lover] eats mine in the Chinese town where I go every night to increase my knowledge of God. I'd like to devour and be devoured by those flour-white breasts of hers." I know Duras writes this seriously—and the narrator thinks this seriously—but there's a playfulness and a lightness to these moments that keeps them from being entirely ridiculous. (Who doesn't want to be devoured by a floury bosom? Come on.)

Knowing that Duras wrote this at seventy, I feel it's just as much about how painful it is to look back at your life in old age and realize how different things can seem. It's also, I think, a story about the mental illness of a parent, especially the kind of mental illness that is only obvious with hindsight or from a distance or which can only be understood when we are more mature. The narrator says: "My mother didn't foresee what was going to become of us as a result of witnessing her despair." Even before her mother attacks her and accuses her of being a prostitute, there are signs of aggression and hallucination. The mother occupies a respectable role in society, but at home she is under intense pressure and struggles to show love and acceptance to her children: "Quite late in life I'm still afraid of seeing a certain state of my mother's—I still don't name it—get so much worse that she'll have to be parted from her children. I believe it will be up to me to recognize the time when it comes, not my brothers, because my brothers wouldn't be able to judge." These lines are chilling, where the distance between the fictional narrator and Duras completely collapses.

Clearly the mother in the novel—who is surely the same as the mother in real life—had, at best, her foibles. Duras herself describes her as "mad." There is an incredible passage where she describes how her mother took over a château when she returned to France and decided to give over a floor of it to the raising of chickens. She bought a job lot of incubators and began to breed them. But something went wrong, all of the chicks' jaws were deformed, and they all starved to death. The stench of their rotting flesh fills the château, and Duras cannot eat in the house without feeling sick. It's heartbreaking.

There is an extraordinary scene where as a child Marguerite sees her mother as a completely different person. Everything is normal, her mother is sitting gazing at the garden, and yet as she looks at her mother's face, it's as if there has been what she calls "a substitution." As if her mother has been replaced by another person entirely. It is a very "writerly" moment, and it makes her cry out in shock and fear. Suddenly she realizes that not only is her mother a stranger to her but also that she is able to stand outside her own life and see it, as if looking in on it from afar.

What sings out of *L'Amant* is the casual cruelty. The way that her brothers never speak to her lover or look him in the eye, even as he pays for their restaurant meals. The fifty thousand francs her brother steals, which is never mentioned again. The rape of the maid named Do by one of the brothers, which is noted—horrifically—in passing. There is something incredibly powerful and brutal about the fragmentary nature of these details. In real life, we remember things without wanting to remember them, and we remember them only in part. We do not have novelistic recall for things exactly as they happened, and often if they were traumatic, our memory barely allows us to remember them at all. (Which is why everyone is always so brutal toward memoirs that paint everything so exactly, including word-for-word dialogue. How could you remember so much?) Duras seems almost aware of this and so structures what is basically a memoir as a novel. She cannot be accused of making things up in a novel. And yet this is as close to a true memoir as anything I've ever read.

For me, everything surrounding this book—and Duras's own story—is as mesmerizingly intriguing as it is sad. Duras is tragic. But she is also funny. She has that same energy as Françoise Sagan: the combination of a death wish and the ultimate celebration of life. For anyone looking for shallow reasons to be interested in French writers (and I'm first in the queue for persons fitting that description), Marguerite Duras was extraordinarily beautiful, and there is some wonderful photography of her as a young woman. I'm aware that this is not a feminist observation to make, but hopefully readers will have realized that I would be just as likely to make this superficial point about an attractive man too. (See the chapter on Maupassant. Swoon.) In pictures she has a striking, disarming gaze and looks fabulously, stereotypically French. And is very similar in appearance to Leslie Caron, who played the title role in the film version of *Gigi*. In a famous photograph of Duras, she is pictured next to her typewriter wearing a V-neck sweater, an unlit cigarette in hand, looking impossibly young and precocious. If you had to conjure up any photograph that represents the stereotype of "the glamorous French writer," it would be this one.

The thing most people say about Marguerite Duras's novels is that they are less about what is being said and more about what is not being said. I always think that idea does her a bit of a disservice. After all, you could say that any book is more about what it is not about than what it is about. This always feels to me like a slightly pointless clever-clever thing to say. Like saying that *Les Misérables* is less about the fate of the lower classes in nineteenth-century France and more about humanity and morality. Or that *À La Recherche du Temps Perdu* is less about memory and more about how lonely and desperate we all feel. Of course, these novels are about both these things at the same time. Every novel has a subtext. For Duras, though, it's fair to say that subtext is particularly key. She is the acceptable and accessible face of the phenomenon called the *"nouveau roman."* The novelists most closely associated with this style are Alain Robbe-Grillet, Nathalie Sarraute, Michel Butor, and Claude Simon. The expression was coined in *Le Monde* in 1957 to mean a new kind of experimental novel, one where the writer redefined his or her style with each book. (It literally means "the new novel.") Alain Robbe-Grillet was to become the thinker behind this genre, establishing the idea that the "old novel" means plot, character, narrative, and ideas, whereas the *"nouveau roman"* centered around objects and the novel emerges from its circumstances. The *nouveau roman* is not afraid of abstract ideas or stream-of-consciousness. It does not rely on coincidences that tie all the threads together. It leaves the threads hanging if it wants to.

I remember trying to get my head around this at university and finding it an incredibly irritating idea. Because obviously these novels were trying to do something a bit different, and obviously they needed to move on from the psychological novels of the nineteenth century and the idea of characters who have things happen to them. But ultimately in order for a novel to work, the reader has to care about the characters in order to want to keep on reading. I was never convinced that the novel could achieve the same thing as, say, a Magritte painting that says *"Ceci n'est pas une pipe"* when it clearly is a pipe. You can understand that kind of thing in visual form. It's far more difficult to maintain that over the word count necessary for a novel. Nonetheless, I don't want to rain all over Robbe-Grillet's very well-established parade. That would be mean. And ill-informed, seeing as he is a great giant of French twentieth-century literature. But all I will say is that I think that Marguerite Duras's *L'Amant* proved that what most readers want is a story about characters they can care about and who feel as if they could be real. Duras became the writer who took this style and made it into something that was both slightly more accessible and slightly more person-alized than the other more academic writers who were her contemporaries. She fused the style of the *nouveau roman* with the narrative expectations of the traditional novel.

Reading back through a lot of the material available on Duras, I am slightly shocked (but not that surprised) to find how she was regarded. She noted herself that her alcoholism was something that was registered differently because she was a woman. It was somehow more disgraceful, more shaming, not the badge of honor that it was for writers like, say, Heming-way. Not that there's anything glamorous about being an alcoholic. But male alcoholic writers of the twentieth century were seen as having a certain allure. Marguerite Duras was not given the same treatment. She was to be pitied to some extent, as a figure of curiosity. During her lifetime people in France were fascinated by her and her work and, on some level, they wanted to support her. She was an exceptionally colorful and popular interviewee. This in turn created her reputation and gave her an audience for her eighteen films and fifty books.

But at the same time, they didn't know quite what to make of her, and the interest in her always had an edge of prurience. After all, what sort of woman really behaves like this?

To put a more positive spin on it, Duras was able to sustain a long and exciting career, packed with the writing she wanted to do, secure in the knowledge that it reached an audience who were engaged. Duras was never someone who was going to write *Harry Potter*, *Game of Thrones*, or a crime series. She wrote obscure, weird literary novels, many of them short and all of them very much not on an epic scale. And people wanted to read them and in huge numbers. She's an awe-inspiring case study for anyone who wants to be a literary novelist. I am not sure that same thing would be possible for any writer now, unless they are a genre writer or someone whose books get made into film or TV. For that reason alone, it is really worth analyzing her output. What would we do with someone like her now? I think even the French-reading public has lost their appetite for a novelist of her caliber and experimental nature.

Happiness is a tricky concept in *L'Amant*, just as it clearly was in Duras's life. It is mentioned occasionally but feels unreliable. The narrator's mother says that her children's infancy and the trips she took were "the happiest days" of her life. But this feels vague and wrong. We know that the days with her children were not happy. The last few paragraphs of the novel are utterly heartbreaking. Without really explaining how or why or when, there is a phone call in Paris years later when he—the lover—calls her. He tells her that he loves her still and will love her until he dies.

The great success of this book is that the lover's love does seem pure and it is the one thing in her life that brings her a sort of peace and sense of being loved, however wrong it is that she is fifteen and he is older. Duras is not one for pulling the morality out of a piece, and she clearly judges neither of them. But the underlying message of it comes across: the harm and cruelty done to this child during her neglectful and confusing childhood is far more painful than the relationship that she had with this man. I read this now very differently to how I read it as a teenager: clear-eyed and sober, able to see the mature Duras who wrote it alongside the child Duras she is writing about. The joy here? When the story is so sad, it's all in the writing: the funny asides, the poetic moments of self-discovery, the feeling of two people in a room together who know they shouldn't really be there and they haven't got very long. Ultimately, though, this book feels like a commentary on forgiving yourself. It's written at the opposite end of life to Sagan's *Bonjour Tristesse*. That is a coming-of-age novel about the happy ignorance of youth. This is a coming-of-old-age novel about coming to terms with that ignorance much later in life. Duras is looking back on her younger self with a range of emotions: nostalgia, envy, regret, joy. If only she had done things differently. If only she could go back to that time. If only we had control over our lives.

7. True happiness may involve quite a lot of hypocrisy: *Madame Bovary* by Gustave Flaubert

(Or: Beware people who dump you by leaving a note in a basket of apricots)

FLAUBERT IS AN author who occupies a certain place in people's imaginations, even those who aren't very familiar with his work. His superficial reputation is probably as someone who thinks about things a bit too much and is a bit too finicky and pretentious. So basically, Flaubert is the ideal nineteenth-century French writer. When the novelist Julian Barnes was shortlisted for the Man Booker Prize in 1984 for his novel *Flaubert's Parrot*, there was a flurry of renewed interest in Flaubert, whom everyone now assumed was a fan of multicolored feathered friends everywhere. In fact, Flaubert only owned a parrot for a short amount of time, and it was stuffed. For people who are irked by pretension around literature and putting fancy writers up on pedestals (readers will already realize I hate this kind of author-worshipping business), *Flaubert's Parrot* is a deeply irritating final straw: it's a book about the futility of trying to pin down "the real Flaubert" while a retired doctor called Geoffrey experiences the futility of trying to pin down Flaubert's real stuffed parrot. (Which, of course, is not a real parrot because it is stuffed.) And all this in a novel that, of course, is not a real story. Exhausting, isn't it, being meta?

My early association with Flaubert was—erroneously—predominantly negative, which is a shame, as I've later come to enjoy *Madame Bovary* as one of my favorite novels of all time. I had never heard of Flaubert when I first saw his name on my university reading list. It was summer. I had just turned eighteen, and I was due to leave home—finally—for the first time in September. I was headed toward the escape I had been planning for approximately thirteen years. And I was headed toward a world where I would be immersed in French for four years. And also in Russian, although at that point I spoke not a single word of Russian. It was usual at the University of Cambridge to choose a language you knew and one you didn't and do a degree combining both. And this was my chosen path in life. Continue with the French I loved. And discover the Russian that I believed reflected my true ancestry. A complicated tussle between the two languages eventually ensued, with Russian briefly winning but French triumphing in the long-term, largely because it's an easier language, France is easier to get to, and they have wine.

Anyway. All that was ahead of me. Before I was to go to university, the French reading list arrived in the post (as email didn't exist). It was about ten pages long and mentioned at least two hundred books. This was the reading list for the first eight-week term. And only for one subject: nineteenth-century French literature. To say that I panicked would be a giant understatement. I had the grades I needed for this university, and I had passed with flying colors, taking extra exams that were optional in order to prove exactly how worthy I was. I was a scholarship girl at my school. I always felt that I had to justify my place, and I wasn't going to take any chances at university either. The reading list, however, was the leveler: I wasn't sure I would belong in this place. And Flaubert's name—a name I had never seen before, despite studying

French for seven years—was the first author listed for week one. I knew nothing of this author. I had none of his books. Worse, the internet had not been invented yet.

I tried not to think about how I was going to read all these books, especially as most of them were French-language editions, and concentrated my efforts on getting hold of any of them at all. This was almost impossible in early 1990s Somerset, where I lived about an hour's drive away from the nearest bookshop—a bookshop very unlikely to stock anything on the list. I already knew none of these books would be in my local library. I have no idea now where my early Flaubert reading ended up coming from that summer. Either I found it in the foreign-language section of a secondhand bookshop or my dad did. My dad was useful for this kind of thing: he was a sales manager for gift companies who supplied department stores, and he was frequently in small British towns with weird secondhand bookshops. One way or another I ended up with two Flaubert novels: *Salammbô* and *La Tentation de Saint Antoine*, both in the original French.

At the time I got hold of these books, I was working as the sole vendor in a bakery called the Crusty Loaf. The baker made bread and cakes all night, and I arrived at eight A.M. to sell them. They got discounted after lunchtime, and anything that wasn't sold by closing time at four P.M. I could take home in black garbage bags to go in the freezer or be eaten. Yes, I put on a lot of weight that summer. Like a human stuffed parrot but without the feathers and much larger. I was on my own behind the counter in the Crusty Loaf and, except for the early-morning rush, it was often quiet and I could read. It was the ideal setup: I was being paid to tackle the reading list, scattering the pages of dusty old secondhand books with flour and doughnut sugar.

Soon, though, my optimism turned to woe. I had hours to myself to get through these books and at least get a head start on the two hundred required tomes. But my attempts to read these books—in French too, as those were the only copies I had—were proving disastrous. I just couldn't get into them at all. *Salammbô* is a historical novel set in Carthage in the third century BC. It was unreadable. *La Tentation de Saint Antoine* is about the temptation of a saint in the Egyptian desert. (To be fair, the title is accurate.) Also unreadable. I would scan the pages frantically, trying desperately to concentrate, wondering if it was because my French was really not that good. Or was it that I wasn't well-read enough and so I didn't appreciate these great works? I became completely terrified. If I couldn't even get through these two, how was I going to approach the other 198?

It turned out much later that I had simply made a rookie error. The university reading lists are guidelines. They are not lists of books to be read. They're comprehensive because they're designed to train you to sniff out your own interests and make your own manageable reading lists. They also have way more than anyone could ever read, as they represent the reading tastes of a broad group of lecturers, some of whom will insist on including *Salammbô*, even if others try to take it off because it is a waste of time. (Truth: it is a total waste of time.) Later on, a lecturer laughed at me: "You're not supposed to read everything on the reading list! That would be impossible!" And I was sad because I had not grown up knowing things like this. Or even knowing that it was OK to ask the question about the reading list. The other reason that the list was so incredibly long, he explained, was that when all the students arrived at university, they would all borrow the books from the library, and the university needed to include enough books so that there would always be something on the list for a student to read.

All this goes to say that by the time I arrived at university, I had not read the most important thing: *Madame Bovary*. I had also failed to understand that this was one of the set texts for that year. Lots of the other reads—including my companion volumes abandoned under the counter of the Crusty Loaf—were simply mentioned for context. I had tackled the context (and failed). I hadn't read the main thing. This meant that I had a week in which to write an essay about a classic novel that I had not read. Within hours a notice appeared on the door of my student room, in my handwriting: "Wanted. Someone who has read *Madame Bovary*." It was partly a joke (and a cry for help). But I also meant it. I needed to find someone who had read *Madame Bovary*. Eventually I did find someone who had read it. Coincidentally, it was the only person in our year who was a vegan. He explained *Madame Bovary* as best he could in the time allowed. He did a good job, but for obvious reasons I failed that paper and was asked to rewrite it for the following term. I learned the hard way how to navigate the reading list and did not make the same mistake again.

Shamed and irritated with myself, I read *Madame Bovary* properly in order to rewrite my essay. But even then I don't remember particularly appreciating it. That came much later, when I reread it at my own leisure and with no essay to write. It's such an extraordinarily beautiful book, especially when you don't read it for the plot. (Although it does have a pretty damn good plot.) Ostensibly this is a book about the inevitable decline of a beautiful young woman, in the same way that *Anna Karenina* is a book about the inevitable decline of a beautiful young woman. But also similarly to *Anna Karenina*, you could give this book another title (*The Life and Times of a French Country Doctor*, for example or even, controversially, *Monsieur Bovary*) and it would be the same book but with a slightly different slant. Our focus is pushed on Emma Bovary—and she drives the narrative—but there are many subplots and other concepts vying for our attention. It's an incredibly rich and complex novel that appears deceptively easy and is always enjoyable. It is particularly recommended for rereading. You find something new in it every time.

The book opens with the story of the exceptionally pathetic husband-to-be Charles Bovary. We know Flaubert is brutal and unflinching from his first, merciless description of "Charbovari." This is the jeering, nonsensical noise the other schoolchildren make when they first hear Charles Bovary stammer his name in front of the class on the first day of school. Is there anything more humiliating than hearing a group of people repeating your name like this? Flaubert is so incredibly mean to Charbovari that it's tempting to imagine that the character represents a person against whom Flaubert has some terrible grudge. When Charles's hat is mentioned, it looks like this: "one of those pathetic objects that are deeply expressive in their dumb ugliness, like an idiot's face." Ouch.

Charles limps along through life but somehow manages to treat Emma's father successfully for his broken leg and, for once, shows himself in a good light. This is pretty much the only time in his life that this ever happens. Charles and Emma are drawn together and marry. Very quickly Emma realizes that she has married an idiot. The truth of this becomes all the more evident after they attend a glamorous ball. They move to Yonville in case it is more exciting there. Spoiler alert: it isn't! Flaubert didn't mean to move them to somewhere that sounds like Yawnsville, but I can't help thinking fate drew him to this idea. Emma is young and beautiful and so starts to harbor warm feelings toward the most attractive man in town, Léon. Nothing happens between them, and Léon is called away to Paris, leaving Emma with a feeling of . . . dissatisfaction.

This feeling soon alights upon Rodolphe, one of Charles's patients, a rich local landowner who likes being bled. They start an affair, which goes on for quite a long time, during which time Emma starts to behave with increasing recklessness, buying scarves and carpets and armchairs and getting further into debt. Rodolphe grows tired of her, especially as she becomes demanding and obsessional. When she suggests they run away together, he dumps her. He does this by leaving her a letter at the bottom of a basket of apricots, which, frankly, is much worse than by text or email. So really these days people have nothing to complain about.

Emma turns to religion and more retail therapy. She and Charles attend the opera in Rouen, where she bumps into Léon. Now that she knows how to have an affair, this time she gets straight to it and before you can say, "What basket of apricots?" she is bouncing across the cobbles of Rouen in the back of a carriage with Léon. Oh, I forgot to say: she has a baby girl (by Charles) while all this is going on and generally pays her as little attention as possible.

In the background Charles is quietly trying to manage his medical practice. Thoroughly unsuspecting of everything going on but disappointed by his wife's lack of affection and general inattention, he decides to perform an operation that will be within his capabilities but still hugely impressive: to cure the clubfoot of a stableboy, Hippolyte. He is cajoled into this by the pharmacist, Homais, an extraordinary and brilliant character in this novel and possibly the true antihero of *Madame Bovary*, deserving of his own novel or at least a sitcom. Homais persuades Charles to undertake this operation, knowing that Charles is likely to bungle it—increasing the prestige of Homais's own illegal medical practice. The operation does go wrong, Hippolyte must have his leg amputated (thankfully not by Charles but by a qualified surgeon), and for the rest of his life, Charles Bovary is haunted by the echo of Hippolyte's wooden leg clomping across the courtyards of Yonville.

The only thing left to happen happens quickly: Léon gets fed up with Emma, and Emma gets fed up with Léon. Her debts mount as she attempts to brighten her life—and her flagging romance—with fripperies and treats. Charles is increasingly unable to meet the debts as his practice sinks further. Seeing no other way out, Emma takes arsenic and dies a horrible, ugly, slow death, with black liquid oozing out of her mouth. (This is my favorite bit of the novel. Even though I like Emma.) After Emma's death, Berthe, her daughter, is sent away and eventually ends up working in a cotton mill. Charles, discovering Emma's infidelities only after her death, is left destitute. The only winner? Homais the pharmacist, who receives the Legion of Honour for his medical achievements.

Madame Bovary is widely acknowledged as a masterpiece of fiction and is credited with completely reinventing the novel. It even spawned a noun in French: *"le bovarysme."* Similar to ennui, this is a tendency toward escapist daydreaming, synonymous with Emma Bovary. I think this is supposed to be something negative and to be avoided, but I can't help thinking that we all need a bit more of *bovarysme* in our lives. Most of all, with his book Flaubert launched a new literary age. Many people have made the claim that Flaubert rethought the novel, bridging the gap between Romanticism and Realism—and paving the way for everyone, from Joyce to Kafka. Closely observed, playful, and rich with psychological insights, Flaubert's novel is assembled painstakingly, and the result is just so incredibly effortless to read.

With *Madame Bovary*, Flaubert showed what the novelist Adam Thirlwell calls "the art of miniaturisation." We see into this microcosm not only of the life of one family but of the mind, passions, hopes, and dreams of one woman. It is the opposite of the grand sweep of history: it is a mind and a memory under a microscope. This feels like a premonition of the world of Freud and psychoanalysis in the twentieth century. In real life, few things make sense and they rarely have a clear beginning, middle, and ending. In the modern novel, life must be described in as naturalistic a way as possible, so as to suspend disbelief. And the way to do this is to miniaturize everything and make connections within that miniature world in the same way that we make connections about our narrative in psychoanalysis.

So that is all the positive stuff. An amazing novel, a superb read, the creation of an unforgettable character . . . Milan Kundera, Henry James, Vladimir Nabokov, and Philip Roth have all hailed *Madame Bovary* as one of the great masterpieces of the ages. It was attacked for obscenity upon publication (mostly because of the bouncing carriage in Rouen), and there was a trial for "outrage to public morality and religion" in 1857. Flaubert, his publisher, and the printer of the book were all acquitted. So there's all that. And then there's Flaubert the man. If you thought that Françoise Sagan and Victor Hugo sounded like complicated people, then it's hard to know where to start with Flaubert. At least Sagan had the excuse of being young (and therefore, as we all are at that age, foolish) when she had a huge, unexpected success with *Bonjour Tristesse*, which, arguably, blighted the rest of her life.

Was Flaubert an insufferably annoying person? Very probably. I am sorry to have to say this about one of the greatest writers of all time, but Flaubert really comes across as a bit of a tit. He went around dressed in black, wearing a white bow tie, even to early-morning lectures at university. If he existed now, he would be a try-hard Instagram influencer who thinks he is Timothée Chalamet but is more like Austin Powers. The writer and critic Deborah Hayden notes that even Julian Barnes—who is totally in love with Flaubert—has his doubts about his great hero. Barnes describes him as "a sweet man"—"unless you count the occasion in Egypt when he tried to go to bed with a prostitute while suffering from the pox."

The novelist George Sand, examining *"le bovarysme"* and Flaubert's tendency toward overanalysis, once said, "This man who is so kind, so friendly, so cheerful, so simple, so congenial, why does he want to discourage us from living?" I cannot believe for a second that she was being serious when she said this. Flaubert could be mean and harsh. But he did have a fantastic flair for one-liners and outlandish ideas, telling his niece just before his death, "Sometimes I think I'm liquefying like an old Camembert." You get the impression that relationships with other people were something that he tolerated and would rather experience from as far a distance as possible. One of the main insights we have into Flaubert's character is thanks to his correspondence with his mistress Louise Colet. I adore how the translator Alan Russell describes their connection as "a sporadic, indeed a largely postal, relationship." If only we could all have sporadic, largely postal relationships.

Flaubert seems to have decided from a young age that he was going to hate everything about life, including his surroundings, his upbringing, and himself. If ever any contemporary writers want to take heart when things are not going well for them, they would do well to Google "Madame Bovary manuscript," where they can find pages and pages of evidence of Flaubert's torture and self-loathing: teeny-tiny black spidery writing accompanied by whole half pages of cross-hatching and crossings-out. He didn't like other people any more than he liked himself. He spent a long time compiling his *Dictionnaire des Idées Reçues* (*Dictionary of Received Ideas*), which was essentially an encyclopedia of human stupidity. His biographer Michel Winock later called this evidence of "an early and profound aversion to mankind." He quotes Flaubert: "I feel waves of hatred against the stupidity of my era suffocating me. Shit is rising into my mouth, as with a strangulated hernia." Speak your mind, Gustave! Don't sugarcoat it! This may or may not have had anything to do with the fact that when he became an adult, he resembled a mournful walrus, with the moustache to match. He seems to have made much less of a big deal of his moustache than Maupassant (mention of whose spectacular moustache is coming to these pages soon), despite the fact that his—Flaubert's—superior moustache would have more than warranted it.

In Flaubert's favor, once he decided that he was going to do something, he stuck at it. It took him five years, writing an average of only five hundred words a week, to complete *Madame Bovary*. Considering that in my experience the laziest novelists write at least five hundred words a day, this is an extraordinarily finicky way to spend your time working fourteen hours a day, often long into the night. I almost cannot bear to think about how he must have agonized over every single word for weeks, months, years on end. It's unimaginable. During this time he became obsessed with individual sentences, crafting them meticulously so that they read as fluidly as possible. He was then extremely annoyed when people told him that his writing was a bit like Balzac's, a writer who was well-known for dashing off thousands of words at a single sitting.

Was Flaubert the most miserable person who ever lived? Or was he actually a misunderstood satirist with a great sense of humor that was just a bit, well, dark? We know that he sat at his desk for up fourteen hours a day. He had an inkwell shaped like a frog. At some point he had a stuffed parrot. Perhaps Flaubert cannot be blamed for his grumpiness as he suffered—just like Dostoevsky, who was also horrifically grumpy—from undisclosed, semi-diagnosed epilepsy. Flaubert's father, a doctor, made sure he was treated accordingly, but neither of them used the medical term, referring instead to "nervous attacks." He also was frequently afflicted with sexually transmitted diseases as a result of his interactions with prostitutes. Reading about Flaubert's medical history, it's a wonder that he found any time for writing fiction at all, as he spent a great deal of time researching treatments for his illnesses, writing letters complaining about them, and having "mercury rubs." (Rubbing a patient with mercury ointment was a common treatment for syphilis.)

There's a lot of evidence that Flaubert, while perhaps not being the most compassionate and generous of souls, was interested in other people and observed them closely. The proof of his sense of humor comes, I think, from the words he puts into Rodolphe's mouth in *Madame Bovary*. Rodolphe is a spectacularly pompous character: "Virginie has been getting decidedly too fat," he says of one of his mistresses, "She's so tiresome, with her wants. And her mania for prawns . . ." This is Rodolphe talking about how to claw his way into Emma's life: "I'll pay them a call or two, send them some game and poultry, have myself bled if necessary." Similarly, Flaubert must have been enjoying himself immensely when he was writing the famous bouncing-around-in-the-carriage scene: he describes the laces of Emma's corset slithering down like adders and the creak of her boots driving Léon crazy.

The evidence of Flaubert's close observation of others is clear from the start of the novel. The description of Charles Bovary's childhood reads like a manual for raising impossible children for parents who couldn't give a damn. Charles Bovary's father insists that the child run around naked "like a wild animal," drink rum as a toddler, and "jeer at church processions." His mother, meanwhile, completely contradicts these actions by tying the child to her apron strings, cutting out paper dollies for him, and feeding him sweetmeats. (I have never understood what sweetmeats are or why any child would want to eat them. They certainly don't bring Charles Bovary any joy.) There is no end of the misery Charles Bovary has to endure in life, whether it's receiving a weekly baked veal from his mother when he is a medical student or being married off to a forty-five-year-old woman from Dieppe with long teeth and large shoes who drinks a cup of chocolate every morning and winds her long, thin arms around him every night in bed. (This is his wife before he marries Emma. Luckily, the long-toothed one dies quickly.)

The mysteries of *Madame Bovary* as a novel have been tying academics in knots for years. There are whole treatises solely on the topic of the meanings of numbers in the novel. You could take these with a pinch of salt if you didn't think about the fact that Flaubert more or less wrote this at the rate of one page a week, a fact that really makes you realize that no single detail can be an accident. The numbers three and four are excessively important, as detailed in a paper by Lynette C. Black. Three represents the spiritual (the Holy Trinity), and four represents the earthly (the four elements). The two numbers (no pun intended, please try to keep up) are often interwoven. There are forty-three guests at Charles and Emma's wedding. Rodolphe is thirty-four. Emma takes forty-three days to recover from her illness. When she tends Rodolphe, her dress has four flounces. Rodolphe pays three francs for the bloodletting. At Emma's funeral, there are three cantors and four rows of candles. Three men carry her casket on three poles, lowering it using four cords. The theory is that the juxtaposition of these two things (the spiritual versus the earthly) is that man never quite gets to transcend his earthly bonds. Before the earthly intervenes, the celestial reigns (when there is still hope): when Charles first sees Emma, she has three bows on her dress; when he first realizes they could have a future, he visits the farm at three o'clock; at Michaelmas he spends three days at the farm; when the young married couple visit the home of the Marquis d'Andervilliers, the invitation is for three o'clock (on a Wednesday, of course, the third day of the week). And, oh yes, the d'Andervilliers' château has three flights of stairs in front of it.

I love all this stuff, by the way, while thinking it slightly ridiculous at the same time. I think Flaubert may have put it all in just to annoy academics and make them speculate pointlessly. When I first learned of this theory, I was preparing my end-of-year exams, had read the book properly, and was thrilled to be able to reread it again, looking out for every single mention of a number. (I highly recommend undertaking a reading this way. It's very rewarding and quite weird.) It was around the time that I found out about the number theory that I must have first discovered the existence of the ridiculous word "leitmotif" and started to use it liberally in my university essays, almost as often as "bildungsroman." Hey, don't you wish you'd known me then? I was so much fun.

Flaubert has also left a mystery to unpick when it comes to the question of feminism in *Madame Bovary*. He gave everyone something to ponder when he said, *"Madame Bovary, c'est moi."* This comment can be taken so many ways. He could mean that there is little difference between men and women and that there is no reason that Emma Bovary cannot be an everyman character. He could mean that he empathizes with the plight of women. He could mean that he identifies with Emma's melancholy nature and flightiness. Or he could mean—and I think this is the most likely thing—that *Madame Bovary* the novel (rather than the character) is about his own view of the world and that it is more autobiographical and more personal than it seems. Nonetheless, there are some surprising feminist moments in *Madame Bovary*. Emma does her hair like a man's. She wears a waistcoat. She smokes a cigarette and tries out Rodolphe's pipe. She attempts—disastrously, but attempts nonetheless—to exert some kind of control over her life and to do what she wants to do, not what is expected of her. She's also very creative with her self-care. You've got to applaud Emma for her attempts at warding off depression. Fourteen francs a month on lemons for cleaning your nails. A blue cashmere dress from Rouen. (I would kill for a blue cashmere dress from Rouen!) A special sash to wear around her dressing gown. Learning Italian. And this: "In certain moods she needed little encouragement to go quite wild." Ultimately these things all lead to her ruin, but I always think that the sign that she is really losing her mind is when she starts making pistachio creams for her husband. No good ever came of a woman making pistachio creams for her husband.

The lesson here is a complicated one. It took me a lot of rereadings to figure out this book. (And I think I still haven't figured it out.) I definitely didn't get all this from the vegan the first time he told me the plot. Certainly Flaubert must have meant to impart some very deep and important message, having taken so much care over the writing of this book. But I don't think he wanted it to be easy to figure out. Ultimately this is a book about the extreme hypocrisy of the human condition. Flaubert wants to portray Emma as a ridiculous, tragic person who deserves to die. She should come across as amoral, untrustworthy, duplicitous. And she is all these things. And yet she is also the most likable character in the entire book. She is honest and transparent in her dishonesty. She wants a better life: she just doesn't know how to get it without doing all the wrong things (such as borrowing money she doesn't have, cheating on her husband, and ignoring her daughter).

Flaubert's argument is that these are the things we are all destined to do ("*Madame Bovary, c'est moi*"). Because we are human, we are earthly, we are idiots. We are trapped in the world of four (the four elements), desperately trying to ascend to the world of the three (the holy trinity). We are doomed to repeat our mistakes. The numbers will never add up for us. Any happiness that is to be found is fleeting and frequently comical. Enjoy your bounce around the cobblestones of Rouen while you can.

It's key that Emma gets her comeuppance. She must die and in an ugly way. She is punished for her attempts at happiness. But I have to wonder: Is Flaubert, even as he punishes her, asking us to question if her fate is just? Did she really deserve this? Because a far worse thing happens in the wake of her death: the pathetic, wheedling, lying pharmacist Homais, who has been portrayed as a piece of work throughout the entire novel, receives the Legion of Honour. This is, I think, Flaubert's ultimate judgment. In this life, the wrong people are punished. And the wrong people are rewarded. Was Emma not justified in her pursuit for happiness, even if it was selfish? At least selfishness is a truthful act.

Despite the complications of Flaubert's character and my initial irritation with his exceptionally weird novels about the desert, no one writes quite like him. There's a scene with Rodolphe where Flaubert makes clear his own views on how difficult it is to express ourselves and say what we want to say, how hard it is to create meaning in a life where there is so little. Only Flaubert—someone who gladly saw the blackness of life—could express this with so much light and depth: "No one, ever, can give the exact measure of his needs, his apprehensions, or his sorrows; and human speech is like a cracked cauldron on which we bang out tunes that make bears dance, when we want to move the stars to pity." The final word on

Flaubert, though, belongs to my friend Alex, a literary critic, who once discovered while transcribing an interview with a writer that an important contradiction about the great author has been brought to light in the digital age: "My voice recognition software has taken 'Flaubert' to be 'flow bear.' Which is amusing. Because he very much wasn't." No, flow bear he was not.

8. Our greatest weaknesses conceal our greatest strengths: *Cyrano de Bergerac* by Edmond Rostand

(Or: Be proud of your huge nose)

IT'S TRUE THAT I have read Proust in the original, have worked for a French-language newspaper, and can conjugate virtually any verb in the subjunctive. I can complain about an order in a restaurant in French while charming the waiter enough to give me a free dessert. And thanks to a 1990s sketch group called Les Inconnus, I can even rap intentionally badly in French. (*"Le rap français, plus fort que jamais / Et si tu comprends pas, c'est que t'es pas branché."* "French rap, stronger than ever / If you don't get it, it's because you're uncool.") However. I have my blind spots. Just as I had a false start with Flaubert, I had a cheat's entry into Edmond Rostand. Neither of the iterations of Cyrano de Bergerac, the seventeenth-century man (a writer and swordsman) or the nineteenth-century play (by Rostand, about the writer and swordsman), were on the part of the university syllabus that I studied. So I picked up all my knowledge of Cyrano mainly through Steve Martin.

I didn't watch *Roxanne* when it first came out in 1987. I was fourteen years old, and somehow it passed me by in that way that films easily passed us by in the 1980s. If you missed it when it was on at the cinema, you would wait a long time until it came out on video. Instead I discovered it a few years later, when I was living in Russia and had been to see a Russian production of *Cyrano de Bergerac* three times. This was pretty typical of how my loyalties toward French had started to wane. Now I was watching French plays in Russian, checking up on my understanding by watching American films and growing tired of French. Perhaps I found a more personal connection in Russian and thought I was accessing my family roots. Perhaps I felt I had learned quite enough French, having studied it for ten years. Or maybe it was because I was a little bit heartbroken, for reasons of friendship, not love.

Not long after I went to university, I had a falling-out with my French pen pal over something I can't even remember now. At the age of nineteen, instead of going to stay with her family, after six or seven years of annual visits, I went to work at a French newspaper for the summer instead. We fell out even more comprehensively when I sent her some copies of articles I had published and she sent back a critique, saying she could tell they were written by someone English. (This was genuinely mean, as they were heavily edited and tidied up by kind French journalists I was working with.) I quit my French-language classes at university and swapped to Russian. I had no interest in Gérard Depardieu's *Cyrano*. I watched the Russian one (played by veteran Russian comic actor Konstantin Raikin). And I watched Steve Martin. Eventually I read it in French, but that was much later, when I had stopped being so childish about my linguistic affections. Looking back, I can see that all this allegiance-switching and identity-questioning hurt no one apart from myself and was all part of a very elaborate ruse to cut my nose off to spite my face. Which is kind of appropriate when thinking of *Cyrano*, as at least there's plenty of nose to cut off.

Cyrano is one of the best creations in comedy, and the play *Cyrano de Bergerac* is the evidence for me that the French know how to have fun, and the silliest of fun at that. Sure, you can see that evidence in Molière too—and I have studied, read, and seen a lot of Molière, including at La Comédie Française, in Paris, the home of truly great French "comedy." I am using the word in quotation marks because it's important to understand the linguistic distinction here. When we say "comedy" in English, we mean something that is funny. That is not so much the case in France, although I would argue that the expression in French has become slightly infected by the English understanding in recent years. However, originally "*comédie*" in French meant something much closer to "theatre" (and this is the case in many European languages, hence "commedia dell'arte"). So the word "*comédien*" in French does not mean "comedian"; it means "actor." The great playwright Molière, author of the original idea of "French farce" then, is "*comédie*" in the French sense. And Molière is pretty funny. But it is not always what we would call "comedy."

Cyrano, however, is funny through and through. Maybe a big nose just translates best into pretty much any language. Steve Martin is the perfect person to channel Cyrano because he has the innate swagger the part demands. He used to do a sketch about being "world traveler Steve Martin, speaking to you from Montreal," where he would say "haute couture" and "haute cuisine" in the most ridiculous (but actually quite accurately French) way: "You see! You learn to speak French by putting a rubber band around your lips," he says, puckering up. See also: "This rare bottle of wine I'm drinking is from a rare bottle of . . . Château . . . du . . . McDonald's." And the bit in a restaurant where he orders in fake French and the waiter tells him he has just requested to massage his grandmother.

"Will there be anything else?" "Yes, get me the telephone. I'm suing my French teacher."

Having discovered *Cyrano* in performance rather than on paper, I was later shocked to find out that Cyrano de Bergerac did not write *Cyrano de Bergerac*. (Have a sit down if this knowledge is shocking you right now.) Edmond Rostand wrote the play *Cyrano de Bergerac* in the nineteenth century. But there was also a real person called Cyrano de Bergerac, who lived in the seventeenth century. To complicate matters, the real-life Cyrano de Bergerac was also a writer, but the one thing he definitely did not write was a play about himself. The Rostand play, which forms the basis of the person we now think of as Cyrano de Bergerac, was written in 1897. The real Cyrano de Bergerac was born in 1619 and died in 1655. But the problem is, we don't know whether Rostand's version of Cyrano is the true story of Cyrano. All of the information surrounding the original, real-life Cyrano is so vast and so conflicting that there are so many versions of him that you might as well assume that Rostand's fictional version is as good as any other.

The play *Cyrano de Bergerac* opened at the one-thousand-seater Theatre de la Porte Saint-Martin in Paris in December 1897 to a sold-out crowd and went on to run for three years. Rostand also wrote plays for Sarah Bernhardt, the great actress of the era. He went on to become the youngest-ever writer to be elected to the Académie française, the national council of letters. He was a good-looking man, a number one winner in any contest featuring French writers with lavish moustaches and no slouch in the selfie stakes. He had a proper circus ringmaster's oiled, twirly moustache reminiscent of Count Olaf in *A Series of Unfortunate Events*, as portrayed by Neil Patrick Harris. But even the spectacular nature of Rostand's moustache could not prevent him from dying early, at the age of fifty, having taken himself off to the countryside "for health reasons"—where he immediately succumbed to a flu epidemic.

Cyrano de Bergerac the play has outlived Rostand's reputation and continues to be revived. The written version of the play is fun to read, not least because Rostand was known for his detailed stage directions. As the play opens, it's clear that this is an unusual setup. It's fair to infer from the first lines of the play that Rostand is a control freak. He describes the set in meticulous detail. It's very rare to read set descriptions or stage directions as clear or as precise as these. "The theatre," Rostand writes, "is a former indoor tennis court, converted and decorated for stage performances." And when Cyrano first appears at the end of scene 3, Rostand tells us it is with "his moustache bristling, his nose ferocious."

Cyrano de Bergerac begins as a play within a play in Paris in 1640 as Cyrano, a poet and legendary swordsman, visits the set at the theatre to challenge the actor Montfleury, who has been banned from appearing. Montfleury intends to go onstage that night, and Roxane, Cyrano's cousin, will be in the audience. We learn that the Comte de Guiche is planning to marry off Roxane to a man named Valvert. Another audience member is Christian, a nobleman, who admits to his friend Lignière that he is in love with Roxane. As you can tell from the setup so far, this is a play where actors can be wandering in and out of the audience, and there are, in a sense, two audiences: the one watching the play in the play (are you following this?) and the actual audience of the play.

As soon as Montfleury appears onstage, Cyrano leaps on and challenges him, dispatching everyone who tries to get in his way. Meanwhile, Christian intercepts a pickpocket and, while threatening him, learns that there is a plot against his friend Lignière. As the crowd is about to leave, the play having been disrupted, Cyrano gets into a fight with Valvert, a duel to the death, with Cyrano ending every sword parry with the line of a poem. He wins the fight, and Valvert seems to have been mortally wounded. Cyrano confesses to his friend Le Bret that he is in love with Roxane. Lignière arrives to tell Cyrano that there's an army of men out to get him, and Cyrano vows to protect him and take them all on.

Cyrano meets Roxane the next day. But before he can tell her of his love, she confesses to him that she is in love with Christian and asks Cyrano to be Christian's protector. Cyrano is now the protector of loads of people. Christian arrives, and a clash with Cyrano almost ensues when he mentions Cyrano's nose (always a mistake). But instead Cyrano embraces him as a friend and tells him about Roxane. Christian is initially happy but then distraught, realizing he isn't poetic enough to keep Roxane's love. Cyrano has the idea that he will woo Roxane on Christian's behalf.

His plan works; Roxane is impressed. Until Christian thinks he can take matters into his own hands and everything starts to fall apart. Then comes the infamous balcony scene, where Cyrano, disguised, seduces Roxane for Christian. Roxane and Christian are secretly married, but when the Comte de Guiche learns of the marriage, he sends Christian and Cyrano to the front lines of the war with Spain. Cyrano writes to Roxane every day, signing the letters as Christian. She comes to the front line to see Christian, who has guessed Cyrano's secret and forces him to reveal it. Just as Cyrano is about to admit the truth, Christian is killed. Roxane never finds out who the real author of her letters is.

Fifteen years later, Roxane is in a convent. Cyrano visits her weekly. One day Cyrano's friends come to tell her that Cyrano has been hit by a log falling out of a window. (Yes, this does seem ridiculous, but it is arguably what happened in real life. And no less ridiculous than many of the other things that have happened.) They are desperate for Roxane to visit Cyrano on his deathbed. Just as they rush off to check on him, Cyrano himself appears. He asks Roxane to read Christian's last letter, and she realizes that he is able to read the letter aloud himself without seeing it. The man she has loved all her life is the man who wrote those letters, and here he is. Cyrano's friends return, and it becomes obvious that this last trip to see his love was always going to kill him. Slashing at the air, making his last marks with his sword, Cyrano dies with Roxane kissing him.

People who know the Steve Martin film will be saying, "Yes, that's great. But where are the firemen?" It's a shame that the Cyrano de Bergerac story has become associated with the film *Roxanne*, because in many ways this film has aged badly. And although the spirit of it—and certainly Steve Martin's performance—is true to the original, many aspects of it diverge, and many aspects of it are peculiarly rooted in the 1980s. In the opening frames, swords and dueling tactics are swapped for horseplay with a tennis racket and ski poles. But the film preserves the dorkiness of the play, which is a good thing. ("You can hide over in that bush over there and I won't see your nakedness. I notice you don't have any tattoos.

I think that's a wise choice. I don't think Jackie Onassis would have gone as far if she'd had an anchor on her arm.")

Arguably the film replaces too much of the cleverness of the original with eccentricity and slapstick. There isn't much point in getting bogged down in the impracticalities of this film because they are often to do with putting Daryl Hannah in uncompromising positions, and presumably that was a good box office move at the time. For example, Daryl Hannah's Roxanne goes naked to the fire station to get help when she is locked out. Steve Martin lets her in her house by climbing into an attic window. (He is improbably athletic.) He then invites himself to stay and makes her a plate of cheese before she can even get back into the house. She is not remotely offended. None of that is in the play.

Roxanne, though, has the exact same spirit of swagger and goodness that infuses the original. It's a particularly exciting movie because it's such a random choice for an adaptation. It fills me with joy that a late-nineteenth-century play based on an obscure seventeenth-century swordsman can be made into one of the most popular, memorable, and also quite mad movies of the 1980s. Martin wrote twenty-five drafts of the screenplay over three years. The best scene is one that mirrors the play closely, where a passerby irritates Cyrano (C. D. Bates in the film) by calling him "big nose." Taking the riff into the territory of "Is that the best you can do?," C. D. counters with twenty self-directed insults that would be more creative. ("It must be wonderful to wake up in the morning and smell the coffee . . . in Brazil.")

There's also a quiet sense of a love of Frenchness in this film that is very sweet. C. D. has a Chagall print above his fireplace. One of his employees at the fire station is reading *Being and Nothingness* by Jean-Paul Sartre. This prompts a scene where Chris—the man Roxanne falls in love with for his looks—picks up the book from the bookshop and the bookseller greets him in French and he is completely clueless. Roxanne simply assumes that Chris has highbrow tastes and is interesting. There's a twist here: C. D. is doubly attractive in the film. (Triply?) He's intelligent and witty. And he knows French stuff. When Roxanne asks him to say something romantic, he does not say, "Why do birds suddenly appear every time you are near." Instead he talks about being "like the blue man in the Chagall hanging over you in a delirious kiss." What bliss. (Just mind the nose.)

One thing worth noting that is common to both the film and the play is the business with pratfalls, which are a tradition of French comedy (and indeed of many forms of European comedy) that is preserved to this day. Stand-up and talky monologue comedy is an Anglo-Saxon thing. It is far more French to fall over as you exit the door, get your nose stuck in the doorway, and then get your hat jammed in the door. (This happens fifteen minutes into *Roxanne*.) There is indeed something joyous and happy-making about this and also, I would argue, fundamentally un-French in the sense that it appears to be unsophisticated. I think one of our stereotypes about the French is that they are chicer, cooler, and more elegant than us and therefore above such things. The truth is, they basically invented pratfalls, and traditional French *comédie* is full of them.

We might not have heard of *Cyrano de Bergerac* if it were not for the dashing actor Benoît-Constant Coquelin. (Coquelin, with its connotations of *"coquin"* [flirty], is perhaps my favorite French surname. Ah, to be Madame Coquelin! Much better than being Madame Cheval.) Edmond Rostand wrote the play especially for Coquelin, and it was arguably his performance that turned it into such a success. Coquelin had acted on stage in the US on tour with Sarah Bernhardt and features in what is thought to be the first film recording made with both color and sound, dating from 1900. As displayed in the surviving film (two minutes long and extraordinary), he was a remarkable portly type with a superbly pompous air about him. Judging from the photographs, this was not just because he was playing Cyrano: he always looked like this. In the short film, you get a measure of the hallmark of French plays of this time: *Cyrano* is written in verse, in rhyming couplets of twelve syllables per line. You can feel the rhythm and cadence of these couplets in Coquelin's performance—and it lends itself brilliantly to Cyrano as a swordsman, as he is able to give a flourish or a parry with his sword to emphasize the rhythm and rhyme of the poetry.

This exists in Shakespeare, of course, and in the poetry and theatre of many languages, but it's particularly beautiful to listen to in French—and it's particularly telling about what was prized in French high society for centuries: the ability to be witty and master the language. Another fantastic example of this is Patrice Leconte's brilliant 1996 film *Ridicule*. It is set later than *Cyrano*, around the same time as the setting for *Les Liaisons Dangereuses*. *Ridicule* tells the story of a well-intentioned minor aristocrat and engineer who is desperate to secure financial support from the court of Louis XVI to drain the swamps in his local area. When he arrives in Versailles, he realizes that the only way to curry favor and attract patronage is to demonstrate wit, or *"esprit."* He learns about the concept of "*l'esprit d'escalier*"—"the wit of the staircase"—the witty thing that suddenly occurs to you on the staircase as you're on your way out. In the court, the most celebrated men are the ones who can demonstrate their wit in rhyming couplets: it's a form of jousting. It would be wrong to suggest that this is still the case in France today or that French culture is somehow more intellectual than others. But the sense of the wit championed by Cyrano is inherent in the language, and in English we have borrowed a lot of these French ideas because we know they don't really belong to us. That is why we say "*l'esprit d'escalier*" and have no expression for this ourselves.

Over time, Rostand has been rather outshone by his big-nosed creation and, in turn, the hero of that play has kept the real-life Cyrano's reputation alive. Real-life Cyrano was quite a character, even if moustache-free. He wrote a series of works about journeys to the sun and the moon that are regarded as some of the first attempts at science fiction and are recognized as featuring the first example of a description of rocket-powered space travel. During his lifetime he was known as a progressive thinker who wrote scores of letters and pamphlets about the possibilities of the future and the idiocies of superstition and witchcraft.

In view of this Michelangelo tendency he had, it always amuses me that one of the most extreme examples of superstition occurred in the district where he was born and not long after his death. As Robert Darnton explains at length in his book *The Great Cat Massacre*, the seventeenth and eighteenth centuries were a time of superstition and myth. People believed in witchcraft and the supernatural. They took these to be perfectly logical explanations for many things they witnessed—and they adopted practices accordingly. Cats, for example, were seen as being in league with the devil and possessing magical qualities. This led to an extraordinary case where a group of workers decided to round up all the cats in the locality, put them "on trial," and sentence them to death by hanging. They acted out the trial in full, killed the cats, and had a hilarious time laughing about this. Then they repeatedly reenacted it all, finding it funnier every time.

This was the atmosphere Cyrano would have grown up in. Where it was common to think that if you buried a load of cats alive in a field, you could be sure that field would have a good yield. If you were ill, you could use cats to cure yourself: drink blood from a freshly amputated tail of a tomcat to heal yourself after a fall; mix your wine with cat feces to fix colic (maybe don't try this for babies); make yourself invisible "by eating the brain of a newly killed cat, provided it was still hot." These were not outlandish or strange things to believe at the time. Certainly there would have been a natural hesitancy around a lot of these practices, and surely the brain-eaters quickly realized that they did not become invisible, but there was very little to suggest that these things might not be true. And if they didn't work, perhaps it was because you had done it wrong or the cat you had chosen was particularly devilish and so had foiled you. Cyrano spoke out against this way of thinking, and that was how he gained his reputation as someone who was quick-witted and able to outthink and outsmart idiots. If only we had him around now.

Both fictional and real Cyrano seem to have shared the giant nose. Cyrano's nose is as much a character as any other player here: "Go, sir, quickly. Or tell me why you're staring at my nose." "I . . ." "Do you see something odd about it? Tell me." Like every comedian since time began, Cyrano wants to be the one to ridicule his flaw before anyone else can do it. Is it like an elephant's trunk or the beak of an owl? he asks. He forces his interlocutor to tell him that his nose is barely noticeable—a speck! This always reminds me of the scene in *Austin Powers* where he is trying desperately not to stare at the mole on the face of the undercover agent named the Mole and ends up shouting, "Moley moley moley!" We all do this all the time, whether with large noses, moles, height (both great and little), big ears, or unusual hair styles, especially wigs.

In the play, Cyrano's three-page ode to his nose is an extraordinary and hilarious thing. It's a way of weaving something beautiful out of self-loathing, a way of turning the most unattractive thing about yourself into the most attractive, a way of turning your enemy's insults upon yourself but improving them so that you seem the more intelligent one. There's also the ultimate nose-protecting warning in the shape of a threat of a duel: "If anyone has any observations / To make about the center of my face / Please note that if he's of sufficient breeding; / I make my mark with steel and not with leather, / And further up the torso, and in front." In other words: Tell me to my face that I've got a big nose and I'll stab you in the heart.

In real life, apparently Cyrano did actually have an absolutely massive nose. This is—pun intended—the centerpiece of this play. Cyrano is, in some measure, deformed by this unusual protrusion. It's his one weakness, the thing that renders him ugly. But it is also the thing that makes him—in his vulnerability—extremely attractive. As the translator Carol Clark has noted, the play is founded on a universal understanding of the insecurity that we all tend to think is unique to us and us alone but in fact is shared by everyone. Clark describes this beautifully as "our belief that we cannot be loved because the qualities that win love are found only in others." If you think about this logically, of course it cannot be true that only the qualities of others are lovable. But it is easy to understand: we all want to be the thing we're not; we all overlook our strengths and write them off as nothing; we all wish we were someone else. This is the curse of humanity. But it's also an extraordinary blessing. It may be hard for us to accept our flawed, repellent selves. But if we can remember that actually other people find us interesting and pleasing thanks to the parts of us that are different, nonconforming, and unconventional . . . Well, that is not only liberating for us all individually, but it is also a sign of humanity not being so bad after all.

Of course, the stereotype—and one that is easily proven to be true—is that we are all suckers for beauty and perfection. And it's pointless denying that. Any Instagram algorithm will bear it out. And no, I don't think Cyrano de Bergerac would have gotten a lot of likes for his selfies. But that is only a part of how we judge people: the superficial reaction. (And, of course, Cyrano is bullied and pilloried in the play and likely was in real life.) The deeper, longer-term reaction that emerges, though, is a heartening one: he is popular, loved, and admired. When it comes down to it, all we really want to do is find an opportunity to see past the surface of things and be slightly better than we are. That is, after all, the main reason why we lose ourselves in books and emerge from that experience refreshed and changed—the opposite of the social media experience, which often leaves us numbed and bored. I'm not saying this to slag off social media completely, as I get a lot out of it and it is a fantastic place to discover authors and books. But if *Cyrano* teaches us anything, then it's about the dangers of superficiality and the benefits of taking the time to see beyond the obvious. There are plenty of opportunities in modern life to forget about that.

It is exactly this quality of self-consciousness that makes Cyrano such a lasting, likable character. He is wonderfully witty and attractive in his own way. We would all aspire to be as articulate and clever as he is. And yet the thing he really wants is to be cute and handsome. It is this very trait, though—of a sort of inevitable self-loathing or, at the very least, self-underappreciation—that makes other people likable to us. People who don't feel this insecurity are desperately unattractive. (In the main. Some people seem happy to vote for political leaders who don't suffer from this quality.)

But this play also does something exceptionally and usually clever: it champions the idea of both laughing at someone because they are ugly while at the same time admiring that person and letting them get their revenge. It's strangely modern. *Cyrano* is about body positivity, and it has an anti-bullying message. Cyrano did not say, "When they go low, we go high." But he could have. The overall philosophy is this: make the most of what you've got and play to your strengths. There is no happier message in a play. It also has a funny kicker: that feeling we've all experienced of not being quite right for someone. Or knowing that we would be perfect for them if only we were thinner, taller, more beautiful, more intelligent, or just a completely different person. As Christian says to Cyrano/ Steve Martin in the film: "Look. She wants somebody who looks like me. And talks like you." You can't be you and still be like someone else. You can't put Cyrano's brain in Christian's head. So just try to be at peace with being you. Play to your strengths, while hiding behind a bush if necessary.

finding a hairdresser who really understands you. I took
my French for granted now and no longer saw the hopes and
dreams that I had had as a teenager as part of my identity. I
was bigger than that now, or so I thought. I would find myself
thinking about French in the way people must think about
a language they spoke with a parent as a child and slightly
resented having spent time on. French? *Bof.*

One thing I never gave up, though, was reading Guy de
Maupassant's short stories, usually in translation. They're just
so easy to read and so enjoyable. They have always brought
me a lot of comfort. One of my happiest memories of my
schooldays is my French teacher, Mr. Harley, reading to us
aloud from translations of Guy de Maupassant's short stories. I
am not quite sure why he did this (rather than teaching a lesson) or whether he was allowed to do this. After all, we were
ostensibly learning nothing, and he was seemingly teaching
us nothing. He wasn't even reading to us in French: he read in
English. He read slowly and deliberately, emphasizing certain
words, chuckling away to himself whenever he found it amusing. But those stories, read aloud to us, once a week or maybe
once a fortnight, were life-changing for me. Perhaps because of
those lessons—where all we had to do was listen—we worked
harder in the other lessons. Perhaps because of those lessons,
we trusted him more, and that made us easier to teach. But
definitely because of those lessons, I learned to love short
stories and to love Maupassant.

Of course, because this was Maupassant, there were
always loads of prostitutes in the stories. I mean, *loads* of
prostitutes. This was probably another reason why Mr. Harley
should not have been reading these stories to a class of
sixteen-year-olds girls at an all-girls school and why a teacher

9. It's all very well to be ambi[tious] as
long as you are willing to pay t[he price]:
Bel-Ami by Guy de Maupa[ssant]

(Or: The bigger the moustache, the gre[ater])

RUSSIAN REPLACED FRENCH in my affecti[ons]
of my twenties. You can't really start a langu[age]
at the age of eighteen—as I had done with R[ussian]
throw yourself into it completely. Now an[d]
holidays would take me to France, and I w[as glad]
that I could speak French. It was always a ple[asure,]
was slightly distanced from the dreams I had
much younger. I thought I would go to univ[ersity]
In the end I spent a year at university in Ru[ssia]
that I would marry a Frenchman. I almost g[ot engaged to a]
Ukrainian but eventually married a man fro[m]

When I went to France as a journalist,
it was to report on stories with a very Brit[ish]
interviewed people on their way out of films b[y]
sial director Catherine Breillat to ask wheth[er they were]
offended by the orgy scenes. (They never w[ere.]
article about being diagnosed by a French "l[ove]
told me that I could attract men by gazing de[ep into their eyes]
and asking them their star sign. (This was [before I met my]
husband. I did not use this on him. He would
are you looking at me funny? You know wh[at my star sign]
is.") I was sent by a magazine to meet Cath[erine Deneuve's]
hair colorist, who revealed that the secret to h[er]

nowadays would not read them. It was highly inappropriate. No one noticed or cared. But, weirdly, when I reread them now, I am amused to find that there is nothing shocking about these stories at all, despite the prostitute-heavy backdrop. Although they frequently mention "ladies of the night" and the lead characters often make financial arrangements with these ladies, there is no detail whatsoever, and we never find out what they actually do together. So while Maupassant is supposedly a bit racy and seedy, in reality he is actually very chaste and innocent.

Maupassant is often seen as a cynical, disillusioned, or pessimistic writer. I completely disagree with this. If you read him at face value in a bad mood, sure. But if you read him in the right mood, he is very funny. Out of all the writers here, it is his writing that actually makes me feel the happiest, which is in itself bittersweet, as he wasn't a particularly happy person. Here's something that will also come as not remotely a surprise: Maupassant had an absolutely massive, lavish moustache. I am not talking about a caterpillar on the upper lip here. I am talking about a tonsorial embellishment that rivaled the hair on his head in terms of prominence (and he had a lot of hair too). Maupassant has a clear-eyed view of humanity and, like grumpy non-flow-bear Flaubert, he had his idiosyncrasies. One of the most important things you need to know about Guy de Maupassant was that he hated having to look at the Eiffel Tower. He wrote that he had to leave Paris because the "metallic carcass" irritated him so much: "Not only could you see it from wherever you went in the city, but you also found it everywhere, made in every material known to man, on sale in all the shop windows, an unavoidable and agonizing nightmare." Before he left Paris, he ate lunch at a restaurant at the foot of the Eiffel Tower because this was the only place in Paris where you did not have to look at the Eiffel Tower.

This, though, was a metaphor for Maupassant's life: a dream can be undone at any moment. It's a good life lesson: be careful what you wish for, because you might get it, but then someone might build a massive tower right through the middle of it. It must have been very strange for people who dreamed of living in Paris their whole lives, who constructed their existence on this dream and moved to Paris in the 1870s (as Maupassant did), to find that they were living in a city dominated by a structure they detested. At least when we visit Paris now, we know the Eiffel Tower is going to be there. Maupassant could not have predicted this. The monstrosity, as he viewed it, was constructed between 1887 and 1889. He had lived in Paris for sixteen blissful, Eiffel Tower–free years. By the time it was being built, Maupassant had been diagnosed with syphilis and had only a few years to live. (He died in 1893.) I can imagine that it must be quite annoying to spend your whole life dreaming of living in Paris and being a literary genius only to find that when you finally manage to have a successful life as an acclaimed short story writer, you have syphilis and have to see the Eiffel Tower everywhere you go. Life is full of trade-offs, isn't it?

My French teacher did not mention anything about Maupassant's syphilis. It is thought that Maupassant contracted syphilis in his twenties. With many writers and artists of the period, there was reference to "the pox," but it was also hugely misunderstood and difficult to diagnose, as the symptoms were so varied. Many seemed to have an awareness of the disease and lived with but did not entirely acknowledge it.

With Maupassant, it probably happened because of—as the novelist Flaubert wrote to his friend—"too many whores." But it may also have been congenital: Maupassant's brother died of the disease. Syphilis was rife at this time, and Maupassant was in good company alongside Flaubert, Baudelaire, Manet, Toulouse-Lautrec, Gauguin, and very likely Van Gogh. Maupassant suffered particularly horribly and died a slow and painful death. He would have been aware of the likely progression of this before it started. Maupassant's horror story "The Horla" deals with the syphilitic madness of its protagonist, and it's not difficult to imagine that by 1887, when it was written, Maupassant was very conscious of his illness and its effect. As well as how irritating the Eiffel Tower was. He tried to commit suicide using, first, a gun and, later, a paper knife. Eventually he became possessed by the idea that his brain was going to be eaten by flies.

Before all this happened (but not long before as it all happened very quickly), he wrote the short and rather perfect novel *Bel-Ami*. It's a quick read and a very enjoyable one, charming, sharp, surprising. This is a novel about cynicism, ambition, and power and how they get in the way of ordinary pleasures. Despite Maupassant's worldliness (and he certainly would have had the beginning of the symptoms of syphilis at the very least and you don't get more worldly than that), this novel is infused with a playfulness and a hopefulness that are incredibly sweet. But it's a deceptive read: it flits between optimism and pessimism. At every turn you think the hero will be outwitted, but somehow he always manages to turn things around. There's a wishful thinking there.

The title of *Bel-Ami* (*Good Friend*) is fascinatingly and intentionally ambiguous. (There also seems to be some debate about whether it should be *Bel-Ami* or *Bel Ami* without a hyphen. Ultimately I've chosen to go with *Bel-Ami* as it's how the author wrote it. In modern-day French, I'm pretty sure it looks old-fashioned, and you'd go with *Bel Ami*.) Georges, the hero—or, perhaps, antihero—of the story is a friend to all, known to them as Bel-Ami. In fact, Georges uses friendship and his amiable demeanor to navigate society. But he is also a "friend" in the euphemistic sense: as in "rather more than a friend"—a lover. There's an ambiguity inherent in the French itself here. As a teenager learning French, I was obsessed by the use of *"copain/copine"* and *"ami/amie"* and *"belle amie/ bel ami,"* the words used to denote "boyfriend/girlfriend." I always found it intriguing that in English you could signal the relationship with someone very clearly by saying, "This is my boyfriend." That is completely different to saying, "This is my friend." In French, though, you might say, *"C'est mon ami"* while meaning, "He is my boyfriend." Or it could equally mean, "He is my friend." This drove me mad, and I always wanted to say, "Do you mean 'ami,' as in 'ami' or as in"—here I would adopt a meaningful look—"'ami'?" In French, you don't have to be too particular about these things. After all, you could change your mind tomorrow. In English, we like to know where we stand.

In a similarly ambiguous way, in some English translations, the title of *Bel-Ami* (which could, I suppose, be rendered *The Boyfriend, Our Good Friend*, maybe even *The Nice Friend*) has become completely unambiguous: *"Bel Ami: The History of a Scoundrel."* The idea that *Bel-Ami* is "the history of a scoundrel" is an interesting one. This isn't a novel like *Anna Karenina*, where the (attractive) protagonist is "punished" at the end for their immorality. And Bel-Ami—Georges Duroy—is not portrayed as an unpleasant person. If anything, maybe Maupassant envies him a little bit. It's surprising to me that it has never been recognized as a particularly important book. Maupassant was not a fashionable writer to study when I was at university, and in some ways that has benefited my relationship with him: I've always seen him as someone to read for fun, not because he's "significant." *I'm* not saying that he's insignificant. Just that few academics would put him on the same level as Proust or Flaubert.

The story in *Bel-Ami* fascinates me because we are clearly supposed to see Georges Duroy's rise through society as "corrupt" and "amoral," but the way that it's written, you rather end up admiring him and wishing that you were him. This is Maupassant's trick: he makes us complicit. *Bel-Ami* is set in Paris in and around the offices of a newspaper called *La Vie Française*. Georges Duroy is working as a railway clerk for a measly 1,500 francs a year, having retired from the army after a stint of military service in Algeria. The great pleasure of his evenings? Sausage sandwiches plus two glasses of beer. But he can't always afford that, so he's looking for a change. He contrives to get himself set up with a job at the newspaper with the help of Charles Forestier, an old army friend. The two of them exaggerate Georges's knowledge of Algerian affairs and get Forestier's enterprising wife, Madeleine, to help him write his articles. She is well-connected, intelligent, and calculating and finds ways to introduce Georges to key figures in politics. He begins an affair with a beautiful woman whom he seems to truly love, Clotilde de Marelle.

Meanwhile Charles Forestier becomes ill and leaves for the South of France to recuperate. The relationship between Madeleine and Georges, though platonic, is already complicated, and when Charles dies, she accepts Georges's offer of marriage. Georges's financial fortunes are ever-improving, as is his standing at the newspaper, but he now finds himself being accused of treading on Charles's grave as his colleagues start to call him "Forestier." Plus, everyone knows that Madeleine writes his articles for him. His marriage to Madeleine is strained from the beginning, as he cannot quite understand why she is with him and wants her to admit that she cheated on her (dead) husband and loves Georges more. She refuses. To distract himself from this, Georges slightly stupidly but very characteristically decides to take his boss's wife, Madame Walter, as his mistress. Her husband owns the newspaper, so this is a high-risk enterprise. But Georges always seems to be one step ahead: somehow he contrives to catch his wife, Madeleine, in the act with her lover and nets himself a lucrative divorce—and freedom.

Now single, Georges has the idea of a valuable—and difficult—prize. Not content with having seduced his boss's wife, he now wants to marry his boss's daughter: Suzanne Walter. It's hard to know whether this is the height of chutzpah and cunning or just horrific. I think probably horrific. But from a fictional point of view, you have to think about what it's worth to see the look on the mother's face as she sees her lover walking her daughter down the aisle. Everything works out for Georges, with only one sting in the tail: Clotilde is present at the wedding, and she makes it obvious to him that she expects their relationship to continue, whether he wants it to or not. So much for his free will. His moustache curls angrily on his top lip in the final pages as he marries Suzanne.

One of the most pleasing details in *Bel-Ami*—and one many critics have remarked upon, so it's not just me enjoying this—is the stroking of the moustache. (Not a euphemism.) As Douglas Parmée writes in the introduction to his 1975 Penguin Classics translation, the hero "has the automatic gesture of stroking—perhaps fondling is the better word—his most striking physical feature, his curly auburn moustache." May we all fondle our most striking physical features more often. The moustache features prominently throughout the story itself. With every mention the fabled moustache becomes more outlandish:

> — "he drew himself up, twirled his moustache with a familiar soldierly gesture and swiftly cast his eye round the room over the belated diners like a handsome young man looking for fish to catch"
> — "his crisp curling moustache brushed back over his upper lip"
> — "his moustache was irresistible . . . crisp and curly, it curved charmingly over his lips, fair with auburn tints, slightly paler where it bristled at the ends"

That sure is some moustache. The more you read, the more you feel possessed by the spirit of the moustache. Beware the curly moustache! It will haunt you even when it is far away! "She frantically closed her eyes in order not to see the man who had just left her." (This is the pious Madame Walter, praying in church after confessing her feelings to Duroy.) "She drove him from her thoughts, she struggled against him, but instead of the celestial vision for which she was hoping in her deep distress, she could still see the young man's curly moustache." Oh, celestial curly moustache! It's like the hairy lip caterpillar is a person. Parmée continues: "Here is the exact, telling detail which by reiteration we shall never be allowed to forget; in a sense, Georges is his moustache."

I don't know if it's specifically because of the moustache, but *Bel-Ami* has long enjoyed a connection with the porn industry: a 1976 Swedish film version starred an actor who was in *Deep Throat*. There is a gay pornographic film studio BelAmi based in Slovakia, established by a filmmaker who changed his name to Georges Duroy in tribute to the protagonist of Maupassant's novel. BelAmi's award-winning films include *BelAmi 3D*, *5 Americans in Prague*, and *Frisky Summer*. I haven't watched them, but I like to think of them as having all the fun of Maupassant's life but without the syphilis. There have been several non-pornographic attempts at film adaptations of *Bel-Ami*, most of them ridiculed. The website Rotten Tomatoes gives the 2012 film version starring Robert Pattinson, Kristin Scott Thomas, and Uma Thurman a rare single tomato (a miserable 27 percent satisfaction rating on the Tomatometer) with one commenter mentioning "Uma Thurman rolling around on Egyptian cotton sheets shouting, 'Look at the grain exports to Algiers!'" The most innocent version starred George Sanders and Angela Lansbury in 1947, under the title *The Private Affairs of Bel-Ami*, featuring a film poster with the tagline "All women take to men who have the appearance of wickedness." Even to the 1940s sensibility the theme is illicit sex with "the cad who gets what he wants."

I'm not sure this is the message of the novel at all, though. We see everything through the eyes of Bel-Ami: he is not always to blame for his actions (others are also taking advantage of him), and he often acts out of weakness rather than out of manipulative malice. In most of the "intimate" scenes in the novel, Maupassant immediately pans away from any activity. Where the novel is not centered on Bel-Ami's character development (which is 80 percent of the novel), there is a lot of plot and exposition. Yes, the majority of the book is driven by his relationships with women. But it is not really about sex. I can't help thinking that the reason the novel has been interpreted in this way—especially for cinema—is because of a certain kind of assumption about ooh-la-la Frenchness. People have ended up making this novel more stereotypically French than it actually is. Even the scenes at the Folies Bergère are innocent and more to do with betrayal, awkwardness, and etiquette than they are to do with sex. Perhaps the problem for film versions is Maupassant's ambiguity: he approaches the novel as if it were a short story where he can leave any explicit conclusions unstated, and it's hard to replicate that on-screen.

Really, though, this is a novel about ambition and power—and their opposites: fear and insecurity. And it is—naturally—about personal happiness, fulfilment, and the physicality of pleasure and contentment. Duroy experiences good fortune and happy moments as a physical sensation: he feels replete, relaxed, filled with warmth and a sense of well-being. All he really wants is to be happy, all the time. But it is the thing that is always outside his reach. When he has one thousand francs, he wants fifteen thousand. When he has fifteen thousand, he wants eighty thousand. When he gets that, he is envious of the person who has millions. And he can't remember that he started out earning just over one hundred francs a month. Maupassant lets him get what he wants every step of the way (this is what is almost cruel about this book)—and yet although he always gets what he wants, he is never happy. In many ways he is simply Monsieur #FOMO (Fear of Missing Out), ahead of his time. If he had been around when social media existed, he could have avoided all the exposure to sexually transmitted diseases and just stayed at home and cultivated a large stable of followers on Instagram.

Which reminds me of something. The one thing that does not ring true in *Bel-Ami* is that none of his mistresses ever gets pregnant, and no one contracts a venereal disease. I suspect this was another of Maupassant's attempts at wish fulfilment: he was in the final stages of syphilis when he was writing this and probably wanted to create a world where people could have lots of exciting liaisons without ever having to worry about contracting a disease that could kill them.

There are lots of details from Maupassant's biography that play out in *Bel-Ami*. He was born in a farming village, Tourville-sur-Arques in Normandy, in 1850. Bel-Ami goes on a visit to his parents in Normandy after he marries Madeleine; it's a disaster, and they have to return to Paris almost immediately because Madeleine finds his peasant parents so distressing. Maupassant's family were well-to-do but wished that they were more aristocratic. His mother, Laure, persuaded his father to change the family name from "Maupassant" to "de Maupassant" to give the illusion of nobility. (And this wasn't entirely an illusion, as Maupassant's father, Gustave, had a relative who had been a counsel to the king in the eighteenth century.) In *Bel-Ami*, not only does Georges Duroy come from a place very similar to Tourville-sur-Arques (although he has unreconstructed peasant parents) but he also benefits from a "reinvention" of his name, becoming "Du Roy."

Another significant detail of Maupassant's childhood becomes key for many of his works. When he was eleven years old, his mother formally separated from his violent father. Securing a legal separation was unusual, risky, and brave on her part. This had a twofold influence on Maupassant.

First, his mother became a key figure in his life and—in my view—this inspired many of the female characters in his work, who often have covert agency or "soft" power. Second, he did not regard marriage as an unbreakable contract. In *Bel-Ami*, Georges Duroy knows how to manipulate the law to his own advantage when he wants to affect a divorce. Perhaps most importantly, though, his mother encouraged Maupassant's association with the writer Flaubert, without whom Maupassant might never have been published. Laure's brother was Alfred Le Poittevin, the poet. Flaubert's father was Alfred's godfather. Laure encouraged the connection in an attempt to benefit Maupassant.

Maupassant was expelled from school for being antireligious. By his late teens, though, he was under Flaubert's wing and was being encouraged to write. He moved to Paris in 1871 and worked as a navy clerk. (Not dissimilar to the job Georges Duroy has in *Bel-Ami*.) Flaubert helped him to get published (Maupassant's mother's plan having been successful), and introduced him to people like Turgenev and Zola. In 1880, Maupassant wrote "Boule de Suif," which had a huge effect. In 1883, his first novel, *Une Vie*, sold twenty-five thousand copies in a year, and his second, *Bel-Ami*, published in 1885, was reprinted thirty-seven times in four months. (Any publishers reading this will be swooning. This represents huge success in any era.)

Once Maupassant was under the spell of advanced syphilis, though, it was as if he became another person. According to his medical records, he planted twigs in the ground, expecting them to grow into baby Maupassants. He licked the walls of his room and insisted on keeping his urine, believing it to be made of diamonds and jewels. (I am a big fan of this kind of self-appraisal of one's urine. We're all being encouraged to embrace "self-love" nowadays, and this seems like a good place to start.) In her book *Pox*, Deborah Hayden writes beautifully of Maupassant's final days, describing how the writer in him was clearly still present. He complained bitterly that he had "lost" his thoughts, cried out to others to help him find them, and then finally "glowed with happiness when he thought he had found them in the form of butterflies colored by mood: black sadness, pink merriment, and purple adulteries. He tried to catch the imaginary butterflies as they flitted by."

I prefer to imagine Maupassant how I think he would want to be remembered: as the "good" version of Georges Duroy, an honestly ambitious fool to himself: "Like a sailor who goes berserk when he sets foot on land, a thrill ran through him each time he saw a skirt." There's so much in the portrayal of Georges's character that is perceptive and really stands the test of time. In the early chapters, Georges twice catches sight of himself in the mirror and is surprised and charmed by this handsome stranger who fits so elegantly and perfectly into Paris high society . . . only to realize that he is admiring himself in the mirror. I always wonder what Maupassant's intention is here. Does he mean to say that we are our own harshest critic and that if only we could see ourselves from the outside that we would look better than we think? That when we take ourselves by surprise, we are really far more attractive than we can ever know? Or does he mean the opposite? That we are vain and self-centered and prone to preening and admiring ourselves in the mirror, while anyone observing us (like the writer) would be able to look on and see how foolish we are? The answer comes a few pages later, when he has his first article published in *La Vie Française*. First, he gets a waiter to go out and buy a copy of the paper for him despite the fact that he already has his own copy. Then he sits and reads his own article out loud in the café, chuckling at the good bits. Finally, he leaves the newspaper behind, ostentatiously crying out that other people might want to read it because it has a very good article in it. Later on in the day he buys another copy and leaves it behind in another restaurant.

And if we're talking about truly French expressions of "joie de vivre," then I think Maupassant has it down. He isn't afraid to be sentimental or clichéd. Who else talks about "fresh air which tasted as delicious as fresh bread"? As Madeleine Forestier says at the first dinner Clotilde de Marelle arranges as a double date: "There's no happiness to be compared with the first gentle squeeze of the hands, when the woman asks: 'Do you love me?' And the man replies, 'Yes, darling, I do.'" Over a dinner of partridges, quail, peas, foie gras, and a "frothy" salad, Maupassant writes that they eat "without tasting it properly, without realizing what they were eating, entirely absorbed in what they were saying, immersed in thoughts of love." A few pages later: "They ate without thinking what they were eating."

But Maupassant has depth. The motif of the mirror is used throughout to show how Georges is changing and to ask whether he can still recognize himself—or even bear to look at his reflection. Later, when Georges sees himself in a mirror, it is when he has gone to visit his boss's wife, Madame Walter, having upset Clotilde de Marelle at the Folies Bergère (where she is embarrassed by Rachel, a prostitute he occasionally sees, calling out to him). He is there on the advice of Madeleine Forestier, and let's not forget who she is to him: his colleague's wife, a woman he has decided to seduce in order to revenge himself on Forestier because he won't lend him any money. In this mirror, everything has gone wrong: "He saw a mirror in which people could be seen sitting; they seemed a long way off. Confused by the reflection, he was first of all making off in the wrong direction." The "mirror moments" are the fleeting glimpses of the integrity he is losing. When he receives his promotion at work and is invited to dinner at the Walters', he admires himself in the mirror as he does up his white tie. He is suddenly reminded of his parents at home, two peasants eating their soup, and he feels a twinge of something that might be called conscience.

The mirror appears again when Duroy and Madeleine Forestier are together and have inherited an unexpected—and large—sum of money from Madeleine Forestier's benefactor: "They seemed like ghosts, all ready to disappear into the night. Du Roy raised his hand to illuminate their reflection in the mirror and said, with a triumphant laugh: 'Look at these millionaires on their way.'" And we see that the mirror cannot help but tell the truth when Madeleine Walter looks into it: "She instinctively went to look at herself in the mirror, to see if she were changed by the impossible, monstrous events that seemed to be overtaking her."

It's interesting that a woman is more able to see the truth in the mirror than any of the male characters. Maupassant creates powerful female characters. But he is also harsh as hell. It is always fun to read his brutal descriptions of women too. On Madame Walter: "She was still a handsome woman, although somewhat fat and at the dangerous age when beauty hangs by a thread." Luckily vigilance and face-packs are buying her a bit more time. On a party guest: "A stout lady wearing a low-cut gown, with red arms and red cheeks, pretentiously dressed with an excessively elaborate hair style and such a heavy tread that you could feel the weight of her massive thighs as she moved." (Tell it like it is, Maupassant! Don't hold back!) "The elder sister Rose was ugly, as flat as a pancake and insignificant, the sort of girl you never look at, speak to or talk about."

Bel-Ami is a deceptively light novel at first. But it comes round to some heavy stuff. See, for example, Norbert de Varenne's speech about the meaning of life. Norbert de Varenne is a character who pops up from time to time, an older man who serves as a warning to Georges. He says that old age is painful, as the older you get, the more aware you are that death is creeping up on you. (I didn't say this was going to be an original speech.) He particularly counsels against loneliness ("Get married"). But he also seems to be encouraging Georges to appreciate his youth and ability to have fun. Georges takes it badly: "It seemed to him as if he had just been shown a hole full of dead men's bones into which he would inevitably fall one day." (I find this sentence hilarious for some reason.) Georges doesn't dwell on this three-page morbid soliloquy for long, though, as soon a woman brushes past him and he finds himself lost in the "fragrant scent of verbena and lilies which she left in the air as she passed." Good old Bel-Ami. It doesn't take much to make him perky again: "He went to sleep in a rapture of joy." Again, I'm never sure of Maupassant's point. Does he want to say that de Varenne knows the truth about life? Or is he emphasizing that Bel-Ami has a better idea of how to live and that despair can be easily turned into hope, with a passing whiff of a lady's perfume?

Because of how fun and sweet and complicated this novel is—not to mention how much I love the short stories—I have a warm feeling toward Maupassant. It's desperately sad that he said at the end of this life: "I have coveted everything and taken pleasure in nothing." I find this hard to believe. He had his own private yacht (called *Bel-Ami*, naturally), traveled extensively, and cultivated solitude. In some cases, the solitude was seen as a reaction to his syphilis. (And who can blame him for wanting to nurse that on his own?) But I wonder if it was also something else. He had a lot of friendships in high society in Paris and struggled with these. He was known to be an enemy of the gossip and indiscretion of that world. His solitude was perhaps a way of preserving his integrity. He was someone who did not think of himself as being happy but who actually lived a life that was full of moments of happiness and success.

Maupassant was perhaps one of the most self-aware and clear-eyed authors in this lineup. He was prone to coming out with the most profound, simple, and beautiful quotes about human existence ("There is only one good thing in life and that is love") while also being able to be funny, silly, and rude. He once declared: "The essence of life is the smile of round female bottoms, under the shadow of cosmic boredom." Obviously in our modern #MeToo age he would be vilified as some kind of misogynistic, abusive monster. But he paid a high price for his familiarity with all those round female bottoms, so I can't bring myself to hate him too much for this. He died far too young, at the age of forty-two.

In his outlook and also in his work, he reminds me of his fellow master of the short story, Chekhov, who died at the age of forty-four. Both have a similar view of humanity and understand our tendency to want to view things in black and white and reach definitive answers. Interestingly, both used the format of the short story to show that life is actually played out in a haze of different shades of gray. (Not *those kinds* of shades of gray, although Maupassant would have liked that.) Both lean on the experience of "ordinary" people whose lives cross theirs, Chekhov in his work as a doctor, Maupassant in his work as, er, a regular brothel visitor. They were not writers who locked themselves in a room and attempted to figure out the meaning of life in that room. They looked for the meaning of life in the lives that they encountered—and raced to the page to reflect that in short stories that were deceptively easy to read.

Bel-Ami, while being a very enjoyable romp about high society, conceals a powerful morality tale. Just as Flaubert contrives to make the "sinful" Emma Bovary into the most attractive character on offer, Maupassant creates an everyman in Georges Duroy whom we want to despise but end up rooting for. Maupassant's own loyalties seem very divided here. At times he treats Duroy like a cat with nine lives: this is a rags-to-riches tale of a boy made good. Is it wrong for him to be ambitious, to want what others seem to have been given on a plate? At other times, though, Maupassant shows how Duroy has been corrupted by this world, that any goodness that was once in him has been squeezed out by greed, malice, and envy. And ultimately his view of Duroy is clear: he is doomed to live a miserable life because he gave in to the weaker part of himself. Maupassant's judgment is gentle: he is an observer of humanity, not a moralist. But he is also a crushing realist. You cannot expect to trample over other people without negative consequences. No matter how spectacularly lavish your moustache.

10. Social climbing rarely pays off, but you'll probably want to do it anyway: *Le Rouge et Le Noir* by Stendhal

(Or: Don't flirt with the woman who pays you to teach her children Latin)

ONE THING I NEVER FORGOT, even if I didn't think about speaking French for ages, was the delight I took in learning new words. I had always got a kick out of the amusing little quirks to be found inside the French language. If someone said something interesting or surprising, you were supposed to say *"aba-di-don"* in a dramatic way, which I always thought sounded like Fred Flintstone saying "yabba-dabba-doo." It wasn't until a long time afterward that I asked someone to write down this phrase: *"Eh bien, dis donc."* ("Oh well, say therefore." Or: "You don't say." Or: "Well, I never.") There were many more ridiculous phrases. If you were fed up, you said something that sounded liked "Johnny Marr," the name of the guitarist in the Smiths. (*"J'en ai marre."*) You could pretend that you were being incredibly rude simply by talking about the swimming pool (*"piscine"*). This word, with its connotations of "pissing," is, according to my long-suffering French teacher sister, virtually impossible to teach to teenagers without the entire class falling about laughing. Now, anytime I want to make my own children laugh, I only have to say in a very serious voice, *"As-tu fait pipi dans la piscine?"* ("Have you gone pee in the pool?") and they will be convulsed for a long time. Foreign languages are very useful for this kind of thing.

As I got older, I understood—to my slight disappointment at first—that it doesn't matter how well you learn a language; you are always learning new words. Language evolves, and it trips you up. It does unpredictable things. I was astonished to find out, for example, that the French for #MeToo is not #MoiAussi (literally "me too"). It is #BalanceTonPorc—"out your pig" or "rat on your pig." There is so much going on with that. Not only does the pig belong to you as if you chose him, it's as if you are responsible for his behavior: it's up to you to expose him, to keep him in check. It's the complete opposite to the confessional victim implied by the idea: "Me too, I've had this happen to me." I don't know if it's good, as it implies an exceptionally complicated relationship between men and women. But then, that's very French. It's interesting that the French phrase contains the idea of #NotAllMen implicitly without having to state that. Not all men. Just the pigs.

Two phrases have always haunted me as useful concepts that we don't have in everyday English but which we could use. *"Être bien dans sa peau"* ("to be well in one's skin") means feeling comfortable with yourself. And the thing that unsettles that feeling: *"un coup de vieux."* This means "to suddenly feel old for no particular reason." It literally means "a knock of the old" or "a blow of the old," the word *"coup"* literally being a physical action. It basically describes that sudden feeling when you think, "Oh, I have aged!" Or, "Oh, I really am old now," and it feels as if someone has punched you in the stomach. It's a feeling you can get from a song or from realizing that you don't know the French for "hashtag" (*"mot-dièse"*). And it's a feeling you can get from rereading something you read very differently when you were much younger. *Le Rouge et Le Noir* is the novel that now gives me that feeling.

Some books you read because they make you feel better about yourself. Others accompany you through life as a touchstone as to how you're changing as a person. And if there is one character in the whole of literature (or at least the whole of literature that I have read, which may or may not be representative of the entirety of global literature ever published) who gives me the knock of the old, then that character is Julien Sorel, the antihero of Stendhal's *Le Rouge et Le Noir*. This is a novel that fits perfectly into the category of "Novels You Should Read Repeatedly at Different Points in Your Life to Check In with Yourself About How Much You've Changed." And when I last checked in with Julien, I felt like I was 158 years old.

You know the kind of novels I am talking about: classics that are unchanging because they are, well, classics, and whose plot and characters can give you a steer on your own changing values and outlook. Julien Sorel is exactly one of these characters: you love him, or you hate him. And your view is likely to change as the years pass. He makes me feel old, jaded, and cynical because when I first encountered him, I found him dashing and attractive. On rereading, he's positively moronic and extremely unattractive as a person. So we know what that means. I was a moron and therefore I did not recognize that he was a moron. I guess it also means that at least I am no longer one. Most of the time. The years have passed, and they have made me marginally less moronic. But they have passed, and, boy, do I feel it when I see that character again through these wizened, increasingly short-sighted eyes. No matter how you feel about him, Julien Sorel is an extremely important character in French literature, and *Le Rouge et Le Noir* is a significant novel. This was, perhaps, not immediately evident. One of my favorite phrases associated with Stendhal's work is the following, which says it all: "None of his published works was received with any great understanding in his lifetime." This comes from the Penguin Classics biography at the start of Roger Gard's translation of *Le Rouge et Le Noir*. That is a very short and fairly cruel sentence encompassing a great deal of heartache and meaning. It is a way of saying: "When he was alive, everyone ignored everything he did."

The novelist André Gide summed up the attitude to Stendhal in an essay he wrote in 1929 about the ten French novels he would most recommend. He wanted to include Stendhal, he said, and was torn between *Le Rouge et Le Noir*, *Lucien Leuwen*, and *La Chartreuse de Parme*. Of Stendhal, Gide says: "Prolonged, his company would be deadly to me." Well, that's not very nice, is it? (In the end he chooses *La Chartreuse de Parme* as the better novel. Wrong!) *Le Rouge et Le Noir* has its fans, though, including President Emmanuel Macron, who keeps a copy of it on his desk. It has been noted that his own trajectory is not unlike Julien Sorel's: intelligent, ambitious young man from the provinces who seeks his fortune in Paris. Let's hope that things work out a bit better for him than they do for Julien.

Le Rouge et Le Noir is a novel in the classic nineteenth-century style written before the experimentations of Flaubert and before the sociopolitical sweep of Hugo. It is known, however, for its originality: Stendhal explores the inner psychology of his characters in a way that was rare for the period, and in some ways, he is a contender for inventor of the psychological novel. There is a famous line in *Le Rouge et Le Noir* that is constantly wheeled out as an example of this new kind of writing. It describes the reaction of the children of the de Rênal family toward their new tutor: "The children adored him; he did not care for them; his mind was elsewhere." We take a sentence like this for granted. It gives us insight into Julien's real character. But for a nineteenth-century novel this was unusual: it tells you in a very succinct and matter-of-fact way that this character has a mind of his own. In a less obvious way, this novel is also a precursor for *Les Misérables*: Stendhal describes a man who has no chance up against the system he faces. Unlike Jean Valjean, Julien Sorel has the means by which to "game" the system without having to disguise who he really is too heavily. But still he is held back by his background at every turn. And Sorel's own ideology does not help him. Jean Valjean has a moral conscience, and he is guided by what he feels instinctively is right. Julien Sorel wants advancement. He dreams of Napoleon and the opportunities that his army once offered. He sees the church as being the one place where he can achieve some kind of advancement and respect. All the while Stendhal points out the hypocrisy of the forces surrounding Julien Sorel, foreshadowing the collapse of the Bourbon restoration in the July Revolution of 1830. The interpretation of the meaning of the title has been important in the history of this novel. The "red" is meant to represent the secular world (and/or the military) and the "black" the church, although there are several other theories on the meaning of the colors, including the idea that red represents love or passion and black represents death. Either way, this was not Stendhal's first choice of title. He was originally going to call the novel *Julien*.

The story is told in two volumes. In the first, the adolescent Julien Sorel escapes his difficult upbringing in Verrières in Franche-Comté in eastern France when he is sent to be the Latin tutor in a wealthy family, a connection arranged by the Abbé Chélan. He is the ambitious son of a carpenter and has ideas above his station: his brothers hate him for being a know-it-all. He dreams of romance and love. He wants to meet the beautiful women of Paris and "compel their attention by some famous deed." (Basically, this is the wish of every single one of us. To win love and be acknowledged.) He has a Napoleon complex but in a good way. He dreams of achieving the same things as Bonaparte, by dint of excellent swordsmanship despite the fact that he does not really have any swordsmanship.

His ideas are lofty but half-formed: he learns Biblical passages of Latin by heart not because he has an interest in the Bible or because he has a faith but simply because he knows it will be impressive to people and he knows he can use it to his own advantage. This is immediately proven as soon as he moves in with the family of Monsieur de Rênal. The young tutor catches the eye of the maid, Elisa, as well as the lady of the house, Madame de Rênal. Flattered to be able to pass in high society, Julien is thrilled when it turns out to be relatively easy to start an affair with Madame de Rênal, who seems to enjoy having her arm touched surreptitiously when they are in groups of people. (This is Stendhal's idea of eroticism.) Elisa, envious of the relationship, reveals Julien's secret and the Abbé Chélan sends him away to Besançon, where he is taken under the wing of Abbé Pirard. When this *abbé* has to leave, he makes sure Julien's future is safe by sending him to Paris as private secretary to the house of Marquis de la Mole, a legitimist (a supporter of the Bourbon restoration).

In part two, it's evident that something is going to go wrong for Julien, as he is not really a supporter of the Bourbon restoration. He loves Napoleon, who was displaced by the Bourbons. Also, he is a dangerous combination of naive and arrogant. The Marquis de la Mole co-opts Julien into a plan involving the exiled Duc d'Angoulême. Engaged on a secret mission, Julien is not aware that he is being drawn into a legiti-mist plot. He is distracted by his relationship with Mathilde de la Mole, his employer's daughter. On his secret mission he learns of a romantic technique from Prince Korasoff. It is a technique that readers will be well-versed in: he pretends to be completely uninterested in Mathilde and sets his cap on another woman. Mathilde, of course, falls for this and is now madly in love with him. Despite this, she gets engaged to someone else richer.

In an unexpected twist, Mathilde's father takes pity on Julien because he recognizes that Mathilde is in love. He gives Julien property, a title, and a military commission. Good times! However, he then suddenly receives a letter from the Abbé Chélan. It contains written testimony from Madame de Rênal that Julien is a social climber and an opportunist. Julien, having almost achieved what he wanted all along, takes a gun, goes to Verrières, and shoots Madame de Rênal while she is praying at Mass in church. She is not killed, but he is arrested and sentenced to death. Mathilde attempts to rescue him, and even Madame de Rênal—who still loves him—begs for his release. But now Julien Sorel has gone into full-blown angry teenager and he wants to die.

Then—in another twist and demonstrating why Julien is an idiot—he finds out that he has not killed Madame de Rênal after all and realizes that he is madly in love with her for real and has been all along. Still, he faces the guillotine (which he absolutely doesn't deserve). Mathilde turns up to kiss his severed head. Madame de Rênal dies quietly of grief a few days later. Bad times all round.

If you are thinking, "Well, this seems extremely far-fetched . . . ," then think again. An important thing to know about *Le Rouge et Le Noir* is that it embodies the idea of basing a piece of work on the *"faits divers"* ("diverse facts" or "news in brief"). I loved thinking about this when I first heard about it. I later learned as a young journalist that news in brief items are known on some newspapers as "nibs." So if you came up with an idea that was a good idea but just very short and barely merited a mention, then the editor would say, "Yes, let's put that in. But it's a nib." The use of the nib for inspiration is a common thing among fiction writers of a certain kind and is an excellent answer to give at a literature festival if you are ever asked where you get your ideas from. (Favorite sarcastic writer's answer: "I buy them from the ideas shop.") To say that you got an idea for a novel because of *"faits divers"* makes you sound clever and whimsical. In fact, all it means is that you saw something in a newspaper and thought, "Oh, I could make a novel out of that."

The nib that caught Stendhal's attention was in a newspaper in 1827. It was about a tutor called Antoine Berthet, a handsome young man from a peasant family who had been employed as a tutor by the Michoud family and may or may not have had an affair with the lady of the house. He moved on to another family, the Cordons, and had a relationship with the daughter of the house. For reasons unknown, he then left their employ and went back to shoot Madame Michoud—in church, just like Julien Sorel—and then turned the gun on himself. Both attempts failed, and he was put on trial and sentenced to the guillotine.

You can see from this brief sketch of Julien's character why you would think he was exciting and glamorous if you were a bit young and foolish. And you can also see why I would evaluate him later on, being a much older woman, as a complete idiot. I am talking about my own reading of him here. This reevaluation of a literary character is a function not only of how much I've changed (and thank goodness sometimes for the *"coup de vieux"*) but also of the fact that when we read books when we're young, we read them fast, and we read the book we want to read more than the book we're actually reading. When I read *Le Rouge et Le Noir* for the first time, it was partly out of duty and not pleasure (it was on my French reading syllabus) and I had to get through it quickly in order to write an essay on it. Later in life, I have read it by choice and was able to read it much more as an ordinary reader rather than someone who was trying to analyze what this book had to say about the role of the novel in the nineteenth century. I always think that reading by choice is the purest and best reading of a book. Of course, we have to have set texts at school and at university, and it would be foolish not to. But there's something that is liberating about reading something just because you want to and not because you have to.

The true function of the novel is to help us understand ourselves and understand others, especially in a world where many of us are spending more time with the sort of storytelling delivered to us by Netflix rather than by novelists. And I write that without judgment because I believe all stories are equal and I have derived a great deal of pleasure from on-screen stories. However, I'm not sure that any other medium can interact with our minds in the way a novel does. And if we don't acknowledge this, we risk losing something that is culturally important. Yes, you can rewatch a favorite television show or a favorite film and sympathize with different characters at different times in your life. And you can revisit something on screen years later and see elements of it in a completely altered light. But the great benefit of a novel is that it is a story you hold in your head: you are the screenwriter, producer, casting director, and director. You get to decide the lighting and all the aesthetics. You "see" and "hear" the characters in the light that you want to see them. Of course, the writer—the novelist—is the guiding light. But in some ways, they are simply narrating and shaping the story that you are imagining. They are your guide. But you are the one taking the walk.

It's because of this intensely personal experience that novels can operate as a window into your own soul, one that only you know about. And they can offer extraordinary keys as to how you've changed as a person over the course of your life and the lessons that you—and only you—have learned. So it is for me and Julien Sorel. When I first encountered him in my mind's eye, he was dashing, elegant, clever, charismatic, and wildly attractive. Completely unattainable, naturally. You can imagine me following him through this book while panting and drooling slightly. (OK, I said no judgment, please.) Looking back, my attitude toward Julien Sorel mirrored my attitude toward attractive young French men I was meeting at the time. They were on a pedestal for me: I couldn't get any of them interested in me, no matter how hard I tried. And in that "trying hard" you can now probably see very easily where I was going wrong. Oh, how I cringe. But with hindsight, there was really nothing to be that impressed by. And so it is—precisely—with Julien Sorel. In fact, I was missing the whole point of the novel by being impressed by him. Just as I was missing the whole point of what I needed to be happy in my own life by "trying too hard" with unsuitable, snooty Frenchmen called things like Hervé and Guillaume.

This mirrors two ideas that have been closely associated with this novel. The first is the theory of "mimetic desire," which describes the dynamic between Mathilde and Julien. At first he is not that interested in her. Then he discovers that she has thrown him over in favor of her aristocratic lovers. He then wants her. Similarly, she is not that interested in him. However, when she finds out he is interested in another woman, a widow, and is corresponding with her, suddenly he is extremely covetable. The other idea is a more familiar one—and one we've all been guilty of from time to time: being in love with the idea of being in love. This is definitely something that Julien suffers from.

I now have more time for Stendhal himself than I have for the fictional Julien. Stendhal is usually described by his biographers as being a man who wanted to dedicate his life to the pursuit of happiness but who was thwarted by everyday reality. (Hello. I identify.) Stendhal's birth name was Henri-Marie Beyle. But he liked using pseudonyms. And when I say "liked," I am really understating things. This was a tradition in French literature: Voltaire used 175 pseudonyms. Stendhal called himself Cornichon (the Pickle), William Crocodile, Henri-Clarence Banti, Octavien-Henri Fair-Monfort, Moncigo, and Marquis de Curzay. It has been estimated that he used over three hundred different names, including, when writing his own autobiography, describing himself as Henry Brulard, Dominque, and Stendhal in the same document. I repeat: this was his own autobiography and none of these names are his actual name. I mean, I like a reinvention of the self as much as the next person, but this does seem a slight overreaction to your parents putting a random girl's name in the middle of your name. His best pseudonym, in my opinion, was Louis-Alexandre-César Bombet, which is the kind of name we should all introduce ourselves with when we are very drunk.

This extraordinary habit of renaming led to an academic journal article being published in 2004 by Ralph Schoolcraft with the award-worthy title: "For Whom the Beyle Toils: Stendhal and Pseudonymous Authorship." (I like to think that someone took the day off after coming up with that.) Schoolcraft notes that the first incidence of Stendhal using a pseudonym was when he was eleven years old and he signed a letter to his grandfather with the name of a vicar who was leading a paramilitary youth battalion that Stendhal wanted to join. I feel this is less a pseudonym than the worst example of a kid trying to get out of gym by faking a letter from an adult.

What else do we know about this man who, if you look at his portrait, had that kind of hair and beard style where it looks as if he is wearing a ring of hair around his entire face? According to translator Roger Gard, Stendhal was a funny man who wore a toupee. Stendhal also had precise views on reading and would not have approved of the summaries in this book. Stendhal regarded spoilers as theft, stealing the reader of the experience of reading. (He makes a good point: that you can only read a book for the first time one time. Upon rereading you never quite recapture that experience because you know what is going to happen.) He was clearly a charismatic character and a student of the charisma of others. In the same way that some of us fantasize about being exciting and glamorous enough as to be secretly French, he wanted to be Italian. His dream was to have the words "Arrigo Beyle, Milanese" carved on his gravestone.

One thing in Stendhal's favor is that he does seem to have understood relationships between men and women, and Simone de Beauvoir even praised him for his depictions of women. Despite Julien's downfall in my estimation, I realize many years later than I probably did in fact envisage him as a sort of young Richard Gere (or perhaps Alain Delon), which is appropriate as there is a reference to *Le Rouge et Le Noir* in the screenplay of *American Gigolo* and the character of the gigolo is called . . . Julien. (You did not expect this to be a book referencing *American Gigolo*, did you? Such are the surprises of life.) It is perhaps not surprising I was taken with the idiotic Julien. He is described as "a slight young man of eighteen or nineteen, weak in appearance with irregular but delicate features and an aquiline nose." Weak! Irregular! Aquiline nose! No point in thinking that I'm alone in my weirdness here either (in case that is what you were thinking). "It was less than a year ago that his pretty face had begun to earn him some friendly feelings among the girls." Get in the queue for the idiot, girls! The first time Madame de Rênal sees Julien, she swoons at his extra-curly hair, which he had dipped into the fountain on his way to meet her, because of the heat. This always reminds me of the controversial "wet shirt" scene in the television adaptation of *Pride and Prejudice*, where Elizabeth Bennet finally falls in love with Mr. Darcy when she sees him going swimming in all his clothes in a pond. That bit is not, strictly speaking, in the novel. Julien's wet, curly hair is.

Is this a novel about snobbery and how we thwart our own happiness by being too snooty to see what joy really is?

Stendhal writes in his memoir, "I would do anything to make the people happy but I would rather . . . spend a fortnight of each month in prison than live with petty shopkeepers." Stendhal's views on social mobility were extremely contrarian. He wanted Julien to be able to rise above his station—and he resented the hypocrisy of everyone around him. But at the same time, he himself was a massive snob. Favorite Stendhal fact? He claimed to have read Shakespeare "continuously" between the ages of thirteen and sixteen. Not exactly a plebeian activity.

But overall, I think this is less a novel about social climbing and politics than it is about the tempestuous nature of desire and how we are all prone to thinking we are crazily in love with someone just because they won't look at us. There is a lot in this novel about the fleeting touch and withdrawal of hands and what you can do if you accidentally brush up against the hand of someone that you're not supposed to touch and how you can make them not pull their hand away. There's also the suggestion from early on that Julien Sorel is a bit of a psychopath. There are many foreshadowings of his eventual demise and of him "turning bad." In the same way that when we first encounter Anna Karenina, it is at a train station, which is also the last place we will see her. And at that station, she is present when a man is crushed to death by a train. Similarly, Julien has an encounter on the way to the de Rênal family. He sees a sheet of paper on a prayer desk that mentions the execution of a man with a name very similar to his. And as he walks past the font, the red blinds on the church's windows give the water's surface the appearance of blood. There are signs and portents like this throughout the novel, indicating that Julien—the idiot!—can never see what's in front of him because he is always distracted by his own fantasies of greatness. Stendhal appears to describe a situation that is the opposite of happiness. Perhaps in his own way, he is the best at capturing joy—because he shows us a character who is completely incapable of hanging on to it.

11. If you're going to behave badly, then do it in style: *La Cousine Bette* by Honoré de Balzac

(Or: Use your disappointing looks to fuel a campaign of revenge against your more attractive cousin)

IN MY MID-THIRTIES, I had a lot of wake-up calls in my life. I made big changes in my working life and put to bed a lot of the obsessive ideas I had had about Russia. I stopped traveling to Moscow four or five times a year as I had done for the best part of ten years. I didn't like being away from my family. My life was evening out, and I was becoming a more sensible person, someone who did not need to retreat into a pretend foreign identity in order to feel happy. It was fairly obvious what was happening. I was becoming far more myself—flawed, sometimes boring, sometimes content—and less the amazing but fake person we think we will be when we are teenagers. By this point I had three children, two of whom were learning French at school and were able to order their own *pain au chocolat* in a bakery. And my parents-in-law had bought a little house in the countryside near Duras (yes, that Duras) in the southwest of France. We started to go there on holiday a couple of times a year. This wasn't the Frenchness I had always dreamed of at all: spending time with English people in France was the opposite of my childhood dream. But it felt much more real and meaningful. Because it was. I slowly settled back into the French part of myself I had buried, became addicted to *Star Academy* (France's *American Idol*) and downloaded music onto my phone that I'd forgotten about for years: France Gall, Patrick Bruel, Jean-Jacques Goldman. I no longer ordered *un chocolat* (a hot chocolate) in cafés. I ordered *un grand crème*, a milky coffee, slightly sharper and more sophisticated than *café au lait*.

For every bit that reading Stendhal makes you feel old (and maybe *Le Rouge et Le Noir* is really a coming-of-age novel that you just have to read at the right time), then Balzac can wake you up again. Balzac is not a writer for the young. He is a lifelong project. You need to live a very long time to read even a fraction of what he wrote because his output was so incredibly prolific. This was, of course, because he was profoundly talented. But there was also another reason. Mention Balzac and most people will think of coffee and not *un grand crème* or *un café au lait*. It's fair to think of Balzac as the patron saint of all writers thanks to his prodigious caffeine intake alone. Or maybe he's the earliest hipster. Either way, he's both a brilliant and a terrible advert for coffee-drinking. On the one hand, caffeine made him incredibly prodigious, as he completed more than ninety novels in twenty years. On the other hand, he basically drank so much coffee that he died of it. Out of all the writers in this book, he's the most neurotic, has the most foibles, and is, I think, the most lovably hopeless.

It is generally accepted that it was not unknown for Balzac to drink up to fifty cups of coffee a day. Yes, fifty. This sounds weird to me. How is that even possible? Many have asked this question, and there has been a great deal of research devoted to the potential size of the cups (espresso, surely?), the size of the pot he used, and his coffee-making methods. It's all speculation because we cannot know for sure. We can only go on the accounts of his behavior that he left behind. He wrote about carefully managing and monitoring his intake so that he could push himself over the line at just the right moment. A typical day's routine involved going to bed at six P.M., waking up at one A.M., mainlining coffee so as to work through to eight A.M., then a short nap before waking and getting in another seven hours at his desk. Voltaire was the only writer who could rival Balzac for coffee consumption: his record was supposedly eighty cups in a day. What is wrong with these people?

In the world I grew up in (in rural England), coffee was a very distant and unimportant thing in the 1970s and 1980s. Nowadays, you can get a flat white virtually in the middle of nowhere and it's common for people to joke about their addiction to coffee. When I was a child, though, and first discovering French, coffee was an exotic thing and I associated it solely with France, I think largely because the word *"café"* means both "a café" and "coffee" in French, and I felt that this gave France proprietorial rights over coffee. I realized that there was a coffee culture in countries like Italy and Spain too, but I had experience seeing the French drink coffee and put it at the center of their lives, and so I thought of it as "their" thing. It's strange how we all seem to have imbued many exotic and pleasurable things that could be attributed to the culture of many countries as being French. I mean, it's not like they invented flaky pastries, grapes, or sex, is it? And yet, despite their neighboring countries also excelling in breakfast baskets, fine wine, and romance, somehow the French got the monopoly on everything.

Balzac, then, is a good, pure French example of a coffee drinker whose habits and output seem synonymous with his national identity. I cannot think of an example of a Russian, Italian, or German writer whose habits are associated with something like coffee in the same way. Coffee was to Balzac what cocktails were to F. Scott Fitzgerald. If you read Balzac's essay *The Pleasure and Pains of Coffee*, it's obvious that he treated coffee in the same way that others have treated cocaine or heroin. (Allow me a bit of latitude here, as I am a total square when it comes to proper drugs. I consider cold brew a heady undertaking.) He advised treating the beans in a certain way, doctoring the amount of water added, taking up to three cups in succession, and, finally, drinking strong, cold coffee on an empty stomach.

The food writer Freddie Moore once investigated on Balzac's behalf whether it was even possible to drink fifty cups of coffee a day and estimated that if this were true, then Balzac would have been drinking a coffee every sixteen minutes. Which seems unlikely. Until you consider that he frequently drank three cups in succession. It's not clear where this figure originates from, in any case. I think it's more important to focus not so much on the amount of coffee or the frequency but on the nature of the coffee: what he wanted was the strong stuff so that it would have maximum effect—to keep him awake and keep him writing.

If you're thinking all this coffee sounds horrible, then it's worth thinking about what Balzac was able to achieve using these methods. It is truly extraordinary to think that Balzac wrote *La Cousine Bette*—a novel of over four hundred pages—in two months. It's a novel about hatred, envy, and bitterness. And at its heart is a complete and utter bitch. It's very *Sunset Boulevard*, and it's fabulous. I first read it when I was at university, and I read it openmouthed: it's breathtakingly detailed and, in a strange way, breathy. That's the effect of Balzac's writing: he writes fast, and you need to read it fast. Marguerite Duras was brutal about this effect: "Balzac describes everything, everything. It's exhaustive. It's an inventory. His books are indigestible. There's no place for the reader." I'm the opposite: I love the claustrophobia and the dysfunction of the worlds he creates.

Cousin Bette is an inimitable character, a villainess of the worst kind: mean-spirited, vengeful, small-minded. And yet what a joy she is. Bette's desire for revenge stems from her obsession with her cousin. Adeline is more beautiful and charismatic than Bette. And she has "stolen" the man Bette should have married. Bette seems to conveniently ignore the fact that the man Adeline has married—Baron Hulot—is not someone anyone would want to be married to. The seed of resentment is sown early on, then, and Bette schemes to bring down Baron Hulot, his wife, and their entire family. Because if she can't be happy, then no one can. She enlists Valérie Marneffe, her neighbor, to seduce Baron Hulot and wheedle as much money as possible out of him, all the while knowing that he is all but ruined by his previous mistress, Josépha. Meanwhile Bette develops a maternal/romantic attachment to her upstairs neighbor, Wenceslas Steinbock, a Polish artist, whom she prevented from committing suicide.

When Steinbock comes into the orbit of Adeline's daughter Hortense and they announce they are in love, Bette's fantasy world collapses. And a secondary reason for revenge—and a more urgent one—emerges. With Bette's encouragement, Valérie takes Baron Hulot to the cleaners, while also ensnaring Crevel (Adeline's lover) and Steinbock. (I'll give Balzac major credit for this: he was good at imagining female characters who could make men do anything they wanted.) Valérie Marneffe's husband, Fortin, works in the government department controlled by Baron Hulot. The increasingly impoverished Hulot finds himself forced into promoting his mistress's spouse. Hulot's financial situation is now desperate. As well as abusing his position at work to promote his mistress's husband, he has asked his uncle Johann to embezzle funds. Balzac cleverly builds the house of cards higher and higher, holding off the moment it will come crashing down as long as possible and concealing Bette's role in the web of intrigue when, of course, she is really at the heart of it all. Hortense discovers Steinbock's infidelity. Baron Hulot's professional misconduct comes to light and he is destroyed. And the final blow is a masterstroke from Valérie: she marries Crevel, meaning that she—Bette's creature—will be connected to the Hulot family, and the wealthiest and most influential member of that family. If this seems like a minor victory for Bette, it's not. She dies, not having achieved anything she wanted.

Bette is such a magnetic and memorable character that she has been compared to Shakespeare's Iago in *Othello*, and the novel itself is so wide-ranging and thought-provoking that it has been compared to *War and Peace*. I'm not sure about the second comparison, as Balzac's work is constructed completely differently to Tolstoy's and is far more about psychological portraits of characters within a certain layer of society. Tolstoy operates on a completely different level. (Let me make it clear that I am not saying that one is better or worse than the other. That's not a hill I'm ready to die on. They're just completely different.) What's unique and important about *La Cousine Bette* is the character of Bette. There is no one quite like her. She definitely falls into the category of antiheroines who are so bad they're good.

Many have been fascinated by the character of Bette, and she has been the subject of feminist readings suggesting that she is a powerful example of the androgynous characters Balzac specialized in. She's certainly original and not a "type." *La Cousine Bette* is a delicious portrait of slow-burn revenge that has parallels with *Les Liaisons Dangereuses*. In this respect the character of Cousine Bette is in some ways similar to the character of Marquise de Merteuil: both are examples of unusually subversive female characters. It was known that she was based at least in part on Balzac's mother, which seems extraordinary as she is in many ways repulsive and monstrous. (Although Balzac was not crazy about his mother, so the portrait is not surprising.) I see something very different in Bette, though: I like her. She's a likable "evil" character. Just as the reader becomes complicit in *Les Liaisons Dangereuses*—where we're almost willing on Marquise de Merteuil and Valmont in their dastardly plot—the whole thrill of *La Cousine Bette* is that she is the villainess with a plan. We want to see what happens when her plan is fulfilled. We don't want to see her plan foiled.

It is particularly pleasing to see this kind of character as a woman, as it's unusual. In the twentieth century, perhaps, not so much, and there's an intriguing Hollywood parallel. Bette Davis is said to have chosen her stage name after *La Cousine Bette*. And she has played a number of characters for whom Bette-style vengeance was key, most obviously in *All About Eve*, in which her character is usurped by a younger, more beautiful version of herself. Just as Bette is usurped by Adeline in Balzac's novel, so Broadway star Margo Channing (Bette Davis) is eclipsed by a young pretender to her crown, the ingenue actress Eve Harrington. Perhaps because Jessica Lange stars in both the movie version of *Cousin Bette* (she plays Bette) and plays Joan Crawford opposite Bette Davis in the TV series *The Feud* (in which both women consider themselves to be the diva-like Cousine Bette of the piece), I now can't look at Jessica Lange in anything without thinking about Balzac.

The descriptions of Bette's physicality are also wonderfully entertaining and playful in the novel. As a reader, I feel less repulsed by them than intrigued. And I also tend to second-guess the narrator (or, rather, the writer). Does Bette really look like a monkey? Or is he simply repelled by a forty-two-year-old woman who has never married and chooses to wear clothes she likes rather than clothes that are fashionable? Is he being ironic? Yes, she has eyebrows that join in the middle and a faintly simian face . . . But there are days when we all feel like that. Does Balzac mean for us to be disgusted by her? Is that intentional, so that when we find ourselves empathizing with her outlandishly fiendish plans, we can look at ourselves and realize that we too have something of the *"bête"* (beast) about us? Beastliness is important. We can all be beastly, and we love beastly characters in novels. They are far more entertaining and honest than benevolent characters.

Balzac was, according to Henry James, "a final authority on human nature." Flaubert was a right old meanie about him and was once quoted saying that Balzac would have been quite a man if he had known how to write. (Flaubert really was a basic bitch.) Proust was heavily influenced by Balzac (and loved him), but even he couldn't resist saying that Balzac was vulgar. To be fair, there is plenty of debate about whether Balzac is perhaps more of a historian than he is a novelist. In some ways he is a sort of documentary-maker using the novel form: he documented what was happening around him. There is a lot of snobbery surrounding Balzac's output simply because of the size of it. Could someone really write so much and maintain quality? *La Comédie Humaine*, his ultimate verdict on human nature, consists of ninety-one works confirmed as finished (including novels, stories, and essays), but there are another forty-six unfinished works too. He brought an extraordinary number of people to life in the pages of his fiction. The biographer Graham Robb estimates that the total number of characters that he created across his life amounts to over 3,500. Even in our age of sequels, prequels, and authors as brands, it's hard to imagine someone coming up with a series of novels that runs to ninety-one volumes. Balzac takes the idea of the "novel sequence" to the extreme, but the concept is not unique to him. Later on this trend extended into the expression *"roman-fleuve"* ("novel-river"). Proust's *À La Recherche du Temps Perdu* is the most obvious example of this. The idea of a novel sequence is that the novels are all interconnected in their depiction of a world and in their aim to portray some overarching idea, but they can all be read separately and do not need to be read in sequence. They depict a world inhabited by a vast cast of characters whose actions may or may not be related.

What was the point of all this for Balzac? My own amateur view of *La Comédie Humaine* is that he conceived it subconsciously as a way to keep writing. After all, what better way to convince yourself as a writer that you really need to write the next book? If it is part of a series or a grand design, then you simply must keep working. It allows for a level of obsessiveness, and it gives you the feeling that everything that you are doing is working toward one great, vastly significant whole. (And, hey, isn't this what we all want out of life?) He wrote a ridiculous amount, including more than thirty erotic tales in a form of medieval French that he invented himself so that only he could read them. Yes, you read that correctly. Ah, if only the author of *Fifty Shades of Grey* had known of this linguistic possibility.

One of Balzac's motivations—and perhaps the one that makes him most unusual among nineteenth-century French writers—was his stated interest in understanding the individual in the context of their family history. Seeing as Balzac's own family was so unusual, this makes sense. One aspect of Balzac's biography that might be easy to overlook—since he himself is such a colorful character—is the extraordinary story of his father. Born into a peasant family near Albi in the south of France, Balzac's father, Bernard-François, was the first child of eleven, born in 1746. I don't know what possessed him to do this or how unusual it was that he did it (very unusual, by all accounts), but Balzac Senior persuaded the local priest to teach him to read and write. This allowed him to take a job as a clerk for a lawyer when he was in his teens—and to leave home for Paris. (Again: unusual in the late eighteenth century.) Balzac Junior tells one particular story of his father's early days in Paris: when Bernard-François was living in the house of the public prosecutor in Paris, he was asked to carve a partridge. He had no idea how to do this. (We are to assume that he had never seen a partridge before.) Instead of saying, "Oh, no, please can someone else do it?"—which is an extremely boring and un-Balzacian thing to do—he took up the knife with such confidence and gusto that he cut through the plate, the tablecloth, and the wooden table. For some reason this impressed people.

Bernard-François believed that you could live to a hundred if only you lived the correct way. This meant "chastity in moderation" (I don't know if this means making sure that you had a lot of sex or making sure that you didn't have very much sex) and only eating one pear for dinner. Balzac Junior went in pretty much the opposite direction and was known for his obsessiveness around abundance. He once served an onion dinner consisting of onion soup, onion puree, onion juice, onion fritters, and onions with truffles (according to Robb). He loved pears and had 1,500 in reserve at one time, enough to get his father through four years.

Balzac's view of women and mothers is fascinating, especially in view of the fact that in his work we are a good few decades before Freud. His father, Bernard-François was supposed to have prided himself on the fact that he taught himself how to suckle from a goat as a baby. This was, said Bernard-François, the way of the Greek gods. (Yes, I also did a double-take when I read this. Skills! Although I really don't understand how you would summon the goat over to you and get it to stay there if you were a baby . . . Maybe let's not think about it too much.) Balzac was, like many other children of urban-dwelling parents of the time, sent out to a wet nurse, something that seems to have upset him for the rest of his life as many of his biographers go on at length as to how offended he was with his mother for years on end. This is something I slightly struggle to understand in the biographies of these nineteenth-century writers. Why would you be upset by something that is presented to you as natural? If everyone you know has been wet-nursed, surely you wouldn't feel hard done by? Maybe he was just generally traumatized thinking about his father and the goat. (As I now am.) I wonder if we are putting some of our latter-day sensibilities onto writers by suggesting that Balzac would have felt maternal deprivation as a child. Yes, he said later that his mother "hated" him, but surely this would have had more to do with his treatment as a child and not as a baby. He was sent to a school thirty miles away from home at the age of eight and saw his family twice in six years. Granted, that is probably going to annoy you even if it is presented as completely normal.

Whatever the truth about his relationship with his mother, Balzac had some peculiar ideas about women. He believed himself to have the magical quality of being able to compel a woman to cross a room to kiss him, like a sort of David Blaine of romance. Part of this was down to his ego and his fantasies of greatness. And I'm not knocking these, as it was these fantasies that partly allowed him to become a writer. But part of this was perhaps also influenced by his mother's interest in magnetism, which he took extremely seriously.

You'd think, what with writing a hundred novels in a lifetime that only lasted until the age of fifty-one, that Balzac might be a bit too busy to bother with much else. It is, then, to his great credit as his father's son that he never quite lost his interest in cultivating bonkers business ventures. He hoped to become a processor of slag from Roman mines in Sardinia. And he once hatched a plot to collect twenty thousand acres of oak wood from Ukraine and transport it to France. On his deathbed he urged a relative to go to America to hunt for an undiscovered gold mine, and earlier in life he had decided that he was going to be a pineapple farmer just outside Paris. I cannot imagine Jonathan Franzen doing any of these things, and he has only written five novels.

Balzac's gargantuan life and larger-than-life, prolific output can feel off-putting, which is why I heartily recommend turning to the Jessica Lange film of *Cousin Bette*. I love Hugh Laurie's lugubrious performance in this film. And I rather love this film, although it is quite odd and it departs considerably from the narrative of the book, including killing off one of the main characters in the first five minutes of the film. This film is well worth seeing, as it gives a flavor of the comedy of Balzac, which surely is important for a writer who cares most about the folly of humanity. In this version, Adeline has died, leaving a husband and a daughter, Hortense, plus her brother and sister-in-law—all at the mercy of Bette, who immediately tries to marry the widower. (He declines.) The deathbed scene with Adeline and Bette is hilarious. Adeline: "Countess Cabbage, we called you. But you never minded!" Bette: "A family like ours could only push forward one girl. Your beauty benefited all of us." Adeline: "You tried to drown me." Bette: "An accident." Adeline: "How they beat you . . ." Bette, coldly: "I don't remember."

Jessica Lange plays Bette as an antecedent of Kathy Bates in *Misery*, and Elisabeth Shue plays the actress Bette will use to take revenge on all the men. "Then you will be the axe," says Bette, "and I will be the hand that wields you." (I did say it was fun, OK?) The film basically turns into *Les Misérables* at the end—with a bonkers ending with nuns with bare backsides. (This is the worst spoiler of them all, and I can only but apologize for it.) When this film came out in 1998, Jean Nathan wrote in the *New York Times* of an adaptation of "the sprawling 1847 drama of manners that is one of Balzac's best-known novels."

Sprawling feels like the right word. Balzac was meanly referred to by Robert Louis Stevenson as "an inarticulate Shakespeare." This description is unfair and unkind but, reading this novel, you can sort of see what Stevenson meant. Balzac does not use one word where he could use a hundred. Conversations that could be dealt with in a few exchanges and take place over perhaps ten minutes in real time are recounted in meticulous details and could take over twenty pages. (I'm thinking in particular here of one of the opening scenes, where Adeline, Bette's beautiful older cousin, is bargaining with Crevel for support in marrying off her daughter.) For the uninitiated, Balzac can feel slightly exhausting to read. However, once you settle into his style and the obsessive eye for detail and hunger to recount every nuance of every facial expression and the mining of every conversational tic, and you tune into the depth at which he's operating, it's completely compelling.

This is not the kind of writing where someone spends five days describing an eyebrow; instead, it's much more like the notes a director or a filmmaker might make about what is really going on in a scene. Balzac has an incredible cinematic eye, and there are moments in *La Cousine Bette* where it can feel as if you're in a real-life nineteenth-century reality television show where every character has a camera following them constantly, picking up their every facial expression and their every murmur. The biographer Graham Robb describes Balzac as "the conscientious though disapproving 'secretary' of French society." He dutifully notes it all down, judging everyone while he's at it. Balzac's sprawling writings are perhaps among some of the most useful to investigate in an attempt to understand some of the tensions of our modern, fast-moving era. Balzac was part of the old-world order in France, horrified by the nouveau riche types who were muscling in on the aristocracy, buying up Paris, embracing materialism.

All this industry could not last forever, though. One of the causes of Balzac's death was cardiac hypertrophy: what's described as "a big heart." For the last twenty years of his life, he used this big heart to have an unimaginable romance, worthy itself of a novel. It's a true story that feels curiously modern and almost like something out of the digital age. In 1832, he received an anonymous letter signed *"L'Étrangère"* ("A Foreign Lady"), complaining that his novel *La Peau de Chagrin* was cynical, atheist, and portrayed women negatively. He was so intrigued by this piece of correspondence that he put an advert in a newspaper, begging for the writer of the letter to contact him again. (This always reminds me of "The Piña Colada Song." It also has to be one of the earliest examples of getting someone to be attracted to you by basically feminist-trolling them and accusing them of being a misogynist.)

The woman who wrote this letter turned out to be a married Polish noblewoman named Eveline Hanska. She and Balzac were to enter into a decade-long correspondence. When her husband died 1841, they began a decade-long discussion about whether they should get married (which was complicated because of her financial situation and her daughter's inheritance). They eventually married in 1850. He was to die five months later.

At the time of his death, "caffeine poisoning" was mentioned. In some accounts, (unproven) syphilis is mentioned. At this stage I would be disappointed if it weren't. He was also diagnosed with "overwork," which seems simultaneously a completely fair, reasonable, and self-explanatory diagnosis as well as a horribly ill-advised thing to die of. The doctor who had known him throughout his life specifically said that he had made himself ill by using coffee to keep himself awake when he should be asleep. I think a lot about this: Did Balzac buy himself more time, more hours awake? Maybe he was physically awake for more hours during his fifty-one years than the rest of us are awake for a longer lifetime. Maybe using those extra hours (that he bought, with coffee, at a high price) was a great investment. Maybe he would not have been able to create *La Comédie Humaine* any other way. But arguably his creation, and the method he used to create it, destroyed him. It can't have helped that when he became gravely ill he was at one point treated by a doctor who prescribed putting your feet into the still-moving entrails of "a freshly opened piglet." (It really does amuse me that this was only just over 150 years ago. I wonder what things we are doing now that will look like this in another century.) He died on August 18, 1850, at the age of fifty-one. Victor Hugo was one of the pallbearers at his funeral.

Bette, of course, lives on and seems just as fresh as the day he wrote her. In the novel she gets her comeuppance. It's hard not to love Bette right to the bitter end, even though Balzac signals that she must die at the end of the novel, as a form of punishment. Not only that, but she also has to endure the realization just as she is breathing her last from tuberculosis that her sister is still—despite everything—happy with her husband! All Bette's vengefulness has been for nothing. However, I can't help feeling that Bette does "win" this novel. The entire family gathers around her bed while she is dying and weeps copiously. All the plans she has pulled off have been completely anonymous and unguessed. She has wrecked lives and wrought misery while all proclaimed her to be the "angel" of the family. Balzac, though, is ambiguous to the end: they are neither completely miserable nor is Bette completely triumphant. In terms of fate, you are left to wonder whether any of us have any control over life whatsoever. We may attempt to manipulate things and push events in our favor. And yet they will work out in whatever way they are going to work out. And this may go for us or against us. Bette gets no real satisfaction.

Still, she is my heroine, and I'm often tempted to procure a large yellow cashmere shawl in tribute to her (the "famous" shawl alluded to in the book, which is so contrary to the sophisticated Paris fashions and can only be explained by Bette's "perverse" personal choice). What is fascinating about Balzac is the tension between the rich world that he describes (arguably no writer's world is richer in detail) and the emptiness of the morality at the end of the tale. There are no winners. But, equally, there are no real losers either. This is perhaps why Balzac is one of the most intriguing and exciting of the French writers: his work is so prolific as to be a catalog of life that we can endlessly examine and try to understand. But like life itself, it is probably unfathomable.

12. Freedom matters more than anything: *L'Étranger* by Albert Camus

(Or: Don't take a gun to the beach)

THE OLDER I GET, the more appreciative I feel about the fact that I studied French from an early age. I think the earlier you encounter a language and the longer it has to sink in, the more it stays with you as the years pass, even with very little upkeep. It was also a huge milestone for me to hear my own children learning French and discovering its quirks for themselves: the cycle continues. But it's less weighted emotionally for me as time goes on. When I was younger, it was part of a battle for identity. I've come to terms with that fight now. I don't need to pretend to be something I'm not. I can handle the fact that I will never be French. And that I'll always have a slight catch in my accent when I say *"grenier"* ("barn"—a favorite word for catching out Brits). I don't bring back tins of snails to cook at home to prove how sophisticated I am. Sorry, again, to my parents for doing this. Most of all, I've found a freedom in my passion for this language and this literature. I love it because I want to. I no longer love it because I'm desperate to prove something. It's an easy love, devoid of obligation.

All the time I was learning French, I felt as if I was building up to a moment of belonging. Early on, I suspected the moment was supposed to be marriage to a Frenchman so that I could be forever known as Madame Cheval. I would cook onion-based suppers for him, and he would respond, *"Bof."*

But as the summers passed and the only man who paid any attention to me was the peach-sweatered Cyril, I understood it was not going to happen. Cyril once watched me eat a whole packet of Roquefort (I really love Roquefort) and murmured, "I love watching women eating." To these people I would always be a freak show: a woman who ate (French girls did not eat at that time), who laughed too loudly, and who was obsessed with saying *"Eh bien, dis donc"* like Fred Flintstone as often as possible. I would always be—like the title of the great Camus novel—the outsider.

And so we come to the writer whose expression of happiness is one of the most contradictory. Camus was born in French Algeria and studied at the University of Algiers, so he himself qualifies as an "outsider." Even though he later attained "insider" status in the literary and political community (he won the Nobel Prize in 1957), he always had the status and the outlook of an outsider. This was partly literal: he had experienced life in another place and challenged the idea of a very insular kind of Frenchness. But it was also abstract and philosophical. He saw that we all view ourselves as outsiders at one time or another.

Camus was less interested in a happy life than in a free life, as philosophically the one cannot exist without the other. There doesn't seem to be anything immediately cheering about Camus's novel *L'Étranger*. In itself the title is annoying as it appears to refer to a great many things at once. The word *"l'étranger"* can mean "the stranger," "the foreigner," or "the outsider." And in the context of the story, it's hard to work out who that person is. Are we supposed to think that the "outsider" is Meursault, who commits a crime half out of boredom, half by accident? Or is the man he killed, "the Arab," an outsider? Many elements of this novel are disturbing. It raises more questions than it answers, which you'd expect, seeing as Camus is more of a philosopher than he is a writer. And I mean that in a nice way.

But the amazing thing about *L'Étranger* is that it is a fun read. By that I do not mean that the plot is fun or that it's funny. Although it does have, I think, dark humor. No, I mean that it's playful. You can revisit it as many times as you want and you'll find something different. It's like a little puzzle, where the answer will never quite be revealed, and you know that, but you still go on trying to work it out. Out of all the authors in this book, I think perhaps Sagan and Camus transcend their status as "French writers" more than any others as they have crossed over into "writers you need to read when you're a teenager." So I read this book when everyone reads this book: at the height of "outsider" status, when I was about seventeen and beginning to realize that however much I perfected my French, I would always be an outsider. Strangely, returning to read this in my forties, it did not make me feel old at all (the opposite to Stendhal). It made me marvel at how fresh Camus's writing is and how the story still resonates. It has been analyzed as a stand-in for all sorts of themes: immigration, racism, colonialism, identity politics, sexism, existentialism.

Is it fair to say that Camus is the most likable and normal of all the writers here? I think so. Among the men he is easily the most attractive, and he doesn't seem to have ever attempted to grow a moustache. Yes, as an adult man he had extensive affairs and at one point had to be hospitalized for a nervous breakdown, brought on by the guilt over a woman to whom he'd been unfaithful. His politics were complicated: he supported anarchism toward the end of his life and had mixed feelings about France's control of Algeria. But all in all, he comes across as a nice guy.

He came from a tough background: both his grand-mother and mother were partially deaf, and his father was wounded in the First World War when Camus was a baby. His mother was said to have a vocabulary of only four hundred words. Camus may have grown up to be one of the most famous existentialist philosophers in history (and became a friend and an adversary of Sartre), but he did not develop his ideas or his identity in a Left Bank café in Paris. The family was very poor, but Camus won a scholarship to a lycée and began to distinguish himself as a footballer. Then he contracted tuberculosis at the age of seventeen, which put an end to his promising career as a goalkeeper. I hadn't fully realized the significance of football in Camus's life when I discovered his work, as it doesn't really enter into his writing. But one of my first jobs in journalism was for the men's magazine *Esquire* in London, and very frequently writers would pitch us stories about Camus and football, and I quickly realized that this was a big deal. Camus is basically to nerdy young football-loving men what Sylvia Plath is to neurotic young poetry-loving women.

To recount *L'Étranger* is to make it sound harsh and difficult, which it really isn't. There is a seductive strange-ness about the text, a sort of detachment that makes you feel as if you're reading the story of a dream: it somehow doesn't feel real. I think it's this feeling that allows you to feel some empathy for Meursault. At the start of the novel he has just discovered that his mother has died. She has been living in a retirement home and their relationship is not close; in fact, he appears to have shut her away there. Meursault seems distant at her funeral, doesn't want to sit with her body and doesn't seem grief-stricken. You sense that we are supposed to think there is something wrong with him and that he's not acting "correctly." But at the same time you have the creeping sense that he is acting honestly and authentically and he is just not going through the motions in the way that society expects. This plants a seed: What else would he do if he were acting honestly and authentically? And if he did that, would that be who he really is, or would it be an expression of his inhumanity? It's unclear if he is emotionless, cold, and inhuman. Or actually very human: his mother's death has frozen him.

The next section has the flavor of an Algerian *Bonjour Tristesse*. And just as Sagan said that all fiction is autobiographical, *L'Étranger* was also based on a truth, if not one connected directly to Camus. The story was inspired by a series of newspaper reports about a fight between two French brothers and an Arab. In the fictional retelling, Camus creates a fourth figure as the key—Meursault—who ends up as both narrator and perpetrator. At the start of the novel, Meursault gets himself a girlfriend, Marie, and they go swimming together and to the cinema. (Remember this. We are supposed to think later that he is evil for doing fun things just after his mother has died. I'm clearly a psychopath, as I was just thinking, "Good for him for taking his mind off it.") He meets up with his friend Raymond, who has been dumped by his Algerian girlfriend. He thinks she is seeing someone else. They write to her and hatch a plot: they will take their revenge on her by getting Meursault to seduce her and then reject her. (Remember this. We are supposed to think later that this is proof of their criminal intent. I was just thinking, "She will ignore the letter. They are very childish.") But she doesn't ignore the letter, and now things get complicated. When Raymond meets his girlfriend, they argue, he attacks her, and he reports her to the police. In court, Meursault speaks up for his friend and says that the girlfriend was unfaithful. Raymond is let off with a caution. After this, the girl's brother and some of his friends start following Raymond around.

It's only a matter of time before this turns into an altercation, and sure enough Raymond is injured in a knife fight. Meursault takes a gun from Raymond, to prevent him from doing something stupid. As he is walking on the beach, he comes across the girl's brother lying on the sand, asleep. As Meursault stands over him, he is blinded by the sun, overcome by heat, and sees a flash of a knife as the brother wakes up. Meursault shoots. You might be able to think, "Oh, it was an over-the-top self-defense reflex . . ." But then he shoots him four more times. Later on, he says he was confused and blinded by the sunlight. Not great murder defense, by the way, in case you're ever looking for one.

Meursault is arrested and imprisoned, awaiting trial. The tone of the novel changes: Meursault was a character in a plot. Now he is a man under a microscope. Who is he, really? And why did he act as he did? Evidence is gathered of Meursault's callousness: his lack of remorse, his strange behavior at his mother's funeral, his attitude to his mother before her death. He is repeatedly asked to express remorse for his crime, but he just can't. This part of the novel is the moral tussle, and it really is hard to come down on one side. Yes, Meursault committed a crime and he is going to die for it. But Camus's task is to persuade us to look at what this means about personal freedom.

It might be hard to argue this in a court of law (so don't ask me to), but I think Camus wants us to treat the shooting as symbolic: it was a mix of free will, accident, coincidence, and irresponsibility. The intent cannot be proven. But we are being asked to examine what the real crime here is. Shooting an innocent man? Executing a man whose intentions cannot be proven? Or, if Meursault is not executed, would that be a crime—to leave the death of an innocent man unpunished? To complicate matters, the dead man is not innocent either, really, as he stabbed Raymond. But, then, Raymond attacked his girlfriend. So, in essence, no one is coming out of this well. In some ways, Meursault's true crime is indifference. But can you execute someone for indifference? The added complication in the modern age is the ethnicity of Meursault's victim. Meursault is a white man who thinks he can do anything (as he and Raymond have already shown), including killing an Arab who was protecting his family. This adds a whole other layer to what Camus perhaps intended as an "abstract" question about humanity. Is it really about racism and colonialism?

In my view, we are not supposed to be able to find definite answers to these questions. We are just forced to examine them. Camus makes his intentions clear, though, with the scenes involving the priest, where he is definitely on the side of Meursault. The priest is frustrated that Meursault won't ask God for forgiveness. If he would only ask God for forgiveness, then there would be hope. But Meursault believes this would be a lie and would deprive him of his freedom. He wants to die, and he wants to feel hated at his execution.

In Alice Kaplan's wonderful book *Looking for* The Stranger: *Albert Camus and the Life of a Literary Classic*, she succeeds in piecing together a biography of the book itself, while walking literally in Camus's Algerian footsteps, fueled by baked chickpea pies sprinkled with cumin seeds. She is intrigued by the multiplicity of meanings in this novel and how it can be reread many times and every time you find a different storyline or a different idea. People have read it as a religious allegory, as a criticism of colonialism, as an exploration of the essential pointlessness of the human condition. Kaplan explains the theory that it may even have represented a sort of wish fulfilment ahead of the independence of Algeria in 1962: "The unconscious wish of the French in Algeria—keep the land and destroy the enemy." But it is more than all these things too. It's funny and playful and full of one-liners.

Kaplan examines whether the novel can be separated from the "*fait divers*" that inspired it and what our relationship to that separation means. Is it wrong if we ignore the story this novel was based on (and the fact that the novel writes the Arab victim's name out of existence)? It seems interesting to me that no one really cares about the real-life stories that inspired *Anna Karenina*, *Madame Bovary*, or *Le Rouge et Le Noir*. And yet with *L'Étranger*, it's different. Perhaps because this novel is so much more than a story; it is obviously meant to be read as symbolic, so we feel as if we really need to understand the symbols. I think we also want Camus to be "the good guy." We don't want him to be someone who is defending or excusing a racist. We don't want him to be a flag-waver for French imperialism. We don't want him to be the writer who sympathizes with the murderer and leaves the name of the victim forgotten.

And yet. Camus's entire point is that there is more integrity to representing Meursault's experience fully and honestly than there is to seeing the story from every point of view. I'm guessing that he would argue that it's impossible to see the story from every point of view. Camus isolates Meursault's worldview and forensically examines it. For him to represent the incident in a more rounded way would have completely distorted the philosophical point he was trying to make. In our modern age, we are keen to head toward a more balanced position. To ask: But what about the Arab victim? Certainly the newspaper reports of the time did the original victim a disservice. His family name was reported as Betouil, as Kaplan points out. In actual fact, his family name was Touil, a French name. Misreporting it as Betouil (an Arab name) is a form of racism: it emphasizes his origins. Camus, however, can't be expected to pick up on all this. He intended to write from the point of view of the killer, not of the victim. His focus is on philosophy and what it means to choose to kill someone. It's right that these real-life facts come to light and that the full story is explored. But it doesn't change *L'Étranger* as a piece of work that continues to confuse, delight, and confound us. This is the brilliance of Camus as a philosopher. Logically and morally perhaps we do not want to engage with a man who can kill someone just because he is a bit distracted by the sun and irritated on behalf of his friend—and also, perhaps, a bit bored. But the human part of us (or is it the animal part of us?) understands perfectly how this could have happened. We know that it is inexcusable, despicable even. But we also understand how Meursault could come to terms with it and actually feel a bit better about himself as long as he felt that at the moment of death he was hated. Understood, condemned, dying—but not alone.

Meursault himself is often very (unintentionally?) funny. The scene where the judge is interrogating him has many comical moments thanks to Meursault's habit of relating everything to how hot and uncomfortable he felt at the time, rather than focusing on what was really going on. When the judge asks Meursault to contemplate his faith in God, Meursault is distracted by "some big flies" that keep landing on his face. The judge is not happy that Meursault flatly refuses to believe in God and shouts that Meursault wants his life—the life of the judge—to have no meaning. This is an interesting point: if you reject God (and the idea of eternal life or a life beyond life on earth), then not only are you rejecting the possibility of meaning in your own life, but you're rejecting it for others too.

Meursault has an entertaining way of reasoning with himself while he is listening to the judge. When the judge says that anyone he has ever shown the symbol of Christ to repents and feels remorse, Meursault's only thought is that they would do that, because they are criminals. Then he remembers that he too is a criminal. ("It was an idea I was having trouble coming to terms with.") He then tells the judge that, no, he doesn't really regret having shot a man; he finds the whole thing rather tedious.

One story always stands out for me in any reading of *L'Étranger* (which is, by the way, a very quick read, almost as quick as *Bonjour Tristesse*). In one paragraph, Meursault deals with a newspaper clipping he has found stuck to the underside of the mattress in his prison cell. It tells the story of a Czech man who leaves the village where he grew up to make his fortune. When he returns home twenty-five years later with his wife and daughter, he decides to surprise his mother and sister by checking into the hotel they run as a guest. The man's wife and daughter go and stay somewhere else and plan to stop by the next day and reveal the "surprise." His intention with this trick is to surprise and delight his mother and sister. Imagine, when the mysterious, wealthy guest turns out to be their own flesh and blood! But, of course, he also wants to make a point: he can now afford to be a guest in their hotel. Sure enough, things go to plan: they don't recognize him, and he checks in.

Then, during the night, things take a sinister turn. Supposedly suspicious of such a wealthy man coming to their village, the mother and sister murder him and rob him, beating him to death with a hammer and throwing his body in the river. The next morning his wife arrives and reveals his identity. His mother hangs herself, and his sister throws herself in a well. (Good times, Camus, thanks so much for that.) Meursault loves reading this story. He takes the view that the traveler got what he deserved, as you shouldn't be messing around like that. It isn't analyzed any further, but the point is clear: in some ways the traveler (who is, in many ways, a "stranger" and perhaps the real "stranger" of this novel) got his comeuppance. He wanted to show off and, in some measure, humiliate his family. He wanted to show that he was better than them. On the other hand, the people who really suffer are the wife, the mother, and the sister, who must live with the horror of this tragedy (and, in fact, cannot live with it). The stranger makes the mistake of hubris. The others must face remorse. Meursault, who seemingly has no empathy and no real sense of morality, does not see this. He can only empathize with the man who got killed and views the situation as being his own damn fault.

Meursault is the equivalent of a modern-day serial killer in a TV drama: detached, ironic, bemused. When he goes to his own trial, he chats to the policeman telling him that he isn't nervous; he's just interested in seeing a trial. (Yes, Meursault, but it is *your* trial!) At the trial, Meursault focuses more on whether he will be forced to acknowledge his ambivalence toward his mother than whether he is actually guilty of murder. (He never seems to face up to this.) He is at his most animated as a narrator when he describes the caretaker remembering the two of them drinking coffee and smoking a cigarette when Meursault should have been visiting his mother's body. The caretaker becomes very agitated on the witness stand as he senses the jury and others in the courtroom disapproving of him sanctioning Meursault's behavior. They drank coffee and smoked cigarettes together! "The old man said in an embarrassed voice, 'I know I was wrong to do it. But I didn't dare refuse the cigarette the gentleman offered me.'"

It is at this point that the word "stranger" appears in the text for the first time. "Yes, the Gentlemen of the Jury will indeed take it into account," says the prosecutor, "and they will come to the conclusion that a stranger might offer a coffee, but that a son should refuse it when in the presence of the dead body of the woman who brought him into this world." Later comes an even worse indictment of Meursault's attitude to the world: "Gentlemen of the Jury . . . just days after his mother's death, this man went swimming, began a casual affair and went to see a comedy. I have nothing more to say." This is an interesting point for modern readers: the only "stranger" or "outsider" mentioned in the novel is the man who offers Meursault coffee. Camus leaves it deliberately ambiguous as to who the real outsider is. Is it Meursault? Is it the Arab? Or is it the stranger who offers you coffee at your mother's funeral and then rats you out for drinking it?

Where does Camus's existentialism leave us with the idea of happiness? "Mama often said that no one is ever really entirely unhappy," says Meursault. He finds that he agrees with her as his supposedly "terrible" life in prison is not as awful as he expected and he manages to find solace in the small things, like a shaft of light or the color of the sky. I sometimes wonder if this is really a novel about the human capacity for hope. Even people who are as hopeless and immoral as Meursault can find a way to hope. However, most people interpret the character of Meursault as some kind of harbinger of doom and believe that we must cultivate lives the complete opposite of his in order to be happy and in order to be good people.

But despite the, er, small detail of the fact that he is a racist murderer, I find some of Meursault's worldview likable. He tells it like it is. He is the Larry David of mid-twentieth-century French-controlled Algeria. When the priest comes to him, exasperated, once Meursault has been sentenced to death, they have a conversation about whether it's a good idea to let God into your life, even if you previously haven't believed in him. The priest appears to insinuate that when you are about to be guillotined, you might as well believe in God, as you have nothing to lose. At this point, Meursault is unsure of the outcome of his appeal and the priest wants to reassure him that he has no extra knowledge and that he's not reaching out to him because he knows that the appeal has failed. In any case, says the priest, this is not about being condemned to death. Because we are all condemned to death. Meursault, amusingly, begs to differ. There's condemned to death by virtue of being alive. And there's condemned to death when someone is about to guillotine you imminently: "I cut in and said it wasn't the same thing and, besides, that wasn't any consolation." This is just it. Just because everyone is going to die doesn't make you feel any better about the fact that you are going to die. The final message of *L'Étranger* seems to be that accepting the "tender indifference" of the world is a way to be happy and feel less alone. It's a slightly depressing message and not really the key to happiness. Which is why, in the happiness ratings, Camus has ended up last.

It's interesting that out of all the authors here, Camus's biography paints him as the kindest, most likable, and least socially dysfunctional of them all. Evidence, perhaps, that an interest in football rather than prostitutes improves you as a person. And yet it's Camus who has created the most monstrous character. How can we distinguish between Meursault and Camus? Camus said that Meursault was "the only Christ we need," by which he meant that Meursault was at least someone who was prepared to face death. The story Meursault tells about his father witnessing an execution and being sick afterward is a true story from Camus's father's life. It was clearly something that haunted Camus. Despite Meursault's clear guilt, his lack of empathy, and his apparent callousness, there is nonetheless something weirdly admirable about him. Camus explained it as extreme honesty: "I see something positive about him and that is his refusal, unto death, to lie." Meursault may be a murderer, a criminal, and a racist. But he has integrity. He never pretends to be something he is not. Camus appears to be suggesting that hypocrisy and denial are worse crimes. In 1948, a man tried to use Camus as his excuse for committing a murder. He claimed he had been influenced by the novel. Camus was asked to respond to this and replied that his work "does not consist in accusing people. It consists in understanding them."

This is why I'm a sucker for Camus and, while judging all the other writers harshly for their syphilis, I am willing to ignore all the evidence of his womanizing. He was an exceptionally forward-thinking person who refused to accept that you have to come down on one side or another of an argument or that things are ever clear-cut. The ideas that he introduced about what it really means to be an "outsider" influenced how I felt about my status toward Frenchness. I was going to have to feel at home in the kind of uncomfortable middle ground that Camus loves to investigate. The moment I had hoped for, when I would finally feel that I had "finished learning French" or "become French" or somehow come to the end of that journey . . . that moment would never exist. Instead, Frenchness was going to have to be something that I lived with and dipped into, rather than something that I tried to assimilate and become. I wonder if the ultimate lesson of Camus is the real proof of happiness: it's the human condition to feel like an outsider, and the more comfortable we are with our outsider status, the more we can let go of it and connect with other people.

The story of Camus's death sounds like something out of a novel he could have written. He was killed in a car accident. An unused train ticket was found in his coat pocket. He had planned to travel by train but had accepted the offer of a lift with his friend and publisher, Michel Gallimard, instead. Gallimard died five days after the accident. This has also influenced how I think about Camus. Yes, he understood how complicated it is to be human, how impossible it is to be happy, morally right, and free. I think he was probably pretty grumpy and annoying a lot of the time, like a lot of the writers here. But he was also the sort of person who would accept a lift from a friend rather than take a train journey on his own. That's a good person.

CONCLUSION

Happiness is not feeling that you
have to pretend to be French

ROBERT DARNTON MAKES an extraordinary point in his book *The Great Cat Massacre*. This is the story of the workers from the area where the real-life Cyrano de Bergerac grew up. They're the ones who thought it would be hilarious to hold a mock trial for all the cats in the local area and then publicly execute them. They thought it was so funny that they reenacted it repeatedly for their own entertainment. Darnton argues that it's really important for us to try to understand why the workers of the rue Saint-Séverin thought it was the funniest thing ever. Because then we will truly understand what it means to be someone else—from another country and another time.

This is a tough leap of the imagination for us to make—as we see their behavior as cruel and sadistic. We would never put cats on trial and then kill them ourselves and laugh at the fact that we were doing it. We would just never do that, would we? (I own a fairly evil cat called Julian, and even I can't imagine this.) But what if we didn't see it this way? What if we could see through to the humor that they experienced? What if we became so empathetic toward their experience that we actually felt the way they felt?

I have come to the realization that it's the same with French joy. We're trying to grope our way toward someone else's experience: to live what they're living, to feel what they're feeling. But what if the feelings we have toward French-ness and our obsession with it are as ridiculous as people putting cats on trial and being entertained by that? The most important question to ask is not "How can I be French?" Or "How can I be as happy/glamorous/sexy/life-embracing as a French person?" It's "What is missing from my life that I have adopted the illusion that being French would somehow help?" The killing of the cats made the workers of Saint-Séverin think that they had some kind of agency and control in their lives when they had none. Being obsessed with being French gives me the illusion that fabulousness not only exists but also is attainable for me. These writers have helped me preserve that pleasant illusion. In some ways, it's a harmless act, this French-worshipping. But as I reread these books at an older age, it has also made me realize that it is a rather sad act, one that means you are always dreaming of another life and never quite inhabiting your own. Sometimes that's the thing that makes us happy. Sometimes we need to avoid going too deep into it and losing ourselves.

The novelist Jeanette Winterson describes books as "energy shots, life-jackets, flying carpets, alarm clocks, oxygen masks, weapons, salves." The books I've examined here perform all these functions and can be useful at different times in our lives. I recommend *Bonjour Tristesse* as an elixir of youth to catapult you back to the feelings you had when you were seventeen: the sun feels different on your skin, people are mysterious and exciting, the prospect of love is fresh and uncomplicated. *Cyrano de Bergerac* is an antidepressant, reminding us that we need only realize that others are suffering just as much as we are: anxiety, self-loathing, and longing are all part of the human condition and are even experienced by people who are as intelligent, charismatic, and charming as Cyrano. *L'Étranger* is the slap in the face you sometimes need when you find yourself feeling sorry for yourself, feeling like you're the outsider—when there are others who really are outsiders who might need your help.

Books are about trying to get under the skin of other people—especially people from the past or from another place, whose thoughts and ideas we can never really know or understand. I think this is especially true of foreign literature or literature in translation. It's crucial that we have that window onto other worlds. When we drop into the mind-set of trying to understand the lives and thoughts of others we're borrowing from Robert Darnton's idea of the *"histoire des mentalités."* This is the idea that studying the way people think can be just as valuable as studying events and facts. When considering the history of our mentality toward France—thinking of "we" as those of us who are Francophiles—then it really does say more about us than it says about France. We want somewhere "other" to love, to aspire to, to swoon over. The writers of that country provide us with fuel for our crush. They construct the dream house for us to live in while we eat salted caramel macaroons, real or imagined, or vanilla-scented madeleines, imagined or remembered.

However, in revisiting these authors and these books and examining them up close, I discovered what I had suspected all along: the illusion of joyful Frenchness is a thing inside me. It doesn't necessarily have anything to do with actual Frenchness. Because we all know the truth: France is a place just like any other, populated by flawed human beings, many of whom are boring and ugly. France has rubbish dumps, roadside ditches, stray dogs, and a disturbing number of *"uritrottoirs"* (weird, stinking metal posts in alley-ways that French men are encouraged to piss against). I have many memories associated with France that have shattered the dream over the years, like the dead, fat bluebottle nestling ostentatiously on the top of a cassoulet that I had to return to the kitchen in a disappointing high-class restaurant when my husband and I were on the "road trip of a lifetime" across the South of France. The staff were awful about it ("These things happen. *Bof.*") and it really put me off "top restaurants" for a long time.

We're all familiar with the feeling of being in a suppos-edly perfect place and experiencing something that contradicts that perfection in the most mundane way. One of the low points for anyone visiting France is when you find yourself ordering in McDonald's or Starbucks and saying words that are familiar to you in English but sound ridiculous in French—(*"Je voudrais un* Big Mac, *s'il vous plait." "Donnez-moi un* brownie."). You feel let down and disappointed in yourself that you have ended up in Starbucks or McDonald's, but you have had to acknowledge that on that day and in those circumstances, it really was the only place that you could go. This has happened to me so many times on the road with kids under the age of ten in France. The choice is: go to a restaurant and be overcharged for food they won't eat while everyone in the restaurant gives them the death stare, or to go to McDonald's and have reliable food and be anonymous. It's not a difficult choice to make. In fact, it's no choice at all. But it always pains me. "We are in France! We can't go to McDonald's!" And yet there we are.

As I have gotten older my Francophilia has not lessened—if anything it's growing with age (and, because I live in the UK, it's growing with Brexit). I have found myself wondering why many people who are into France are not really that into French people. France is one thing. French people are quite another. Not everyone who loves France is a French speaker. And even not all France-loving French speakers have any time for French people. This is where these books come in: there's a window into Frenchness, but they're also a way of understanding French people better.

If this sounds odd, then think about how most people—who do not spend very much time in France and who do not speak French—interact with this country: it is a holiday destination, a place for relaxation, romance, shopping, eating. Most people's interactions with French people are with the French who work in the service industry, and please believe me when I say that if you interact only with the service industry (and especially as a foreigner) then you will not receive the best of the French. It is one of my great missions in life to make French people who work in the service industry laugh while they are on the job. This is an act that proves that I can speak French as well as I imagine that I can. And it shows that I can still crack the nut—and, *mon Dieu*, is that a hard nut to crack. (I picture myself saying this as Joey Tribbiani. Still got it. Or, rather, "Flabadou babadadou.")

What I have always wanted—and I think I always thought that the only way I could get it was through literature—was more than a superficial connection with France. It's easy to have a surface connection: to enjoy the food, breathe in the Chanel No. 5, and shrug a lot. Anyone can do that. Indeed, one of the problems with French is that I think we imagine we can speak it a lot better than we can, just by putting on a sexy voice. It is the sort of language that lends itself very well to thinking that the drunker you are, the more fluent you are. But I wanted something deeper and more meaningful: that, for me, was where the true happiness lay, in finding something amazing underneath the upper layer of pleasure. Even when I didn't speak great French and I was reading a lot of French writers in translation, I tended to believe that the more I read what had been created in France by French minds—even if I wasn't reading it in French (or even if I was but not understanding everything)—the more likely I was to infuse myself with Frenchness. I think that has turned out to be true. Immersion of one kind or another is really the only way to feel your way into another culture. You can do it with language by isolating yourself from your mother tongue and throwing yourself in at the deep end. Or you can make sure that your radio is always tuned to a French station. Or you can read as widely as possible—or, rather, as narrowly as possible. As in: make sure you read only French authors for a year. Or ten years.

Why do we foreigners feel we need to do these things? Why are we drawn to another culture? Why don't we just celebrate our own culture and stick with that? Why are we drawn to thinking that someone else's culture is more exciting? Maybe it feels too self-involved or too self-validating to be in love with your own nationality, so you need someone else's to admire. (Although, let's be honest, the French don't seem to have a problem with this.) For me, I think Frenchness represents a lifelong dream that if only for a slightly different accident of birth, I would be a much better person than the person I am: I would be effortlessly slim, have glossy hair and long, tanned legs, and I would have really great taste in clothes, music, art, furnishings, and literature. When I moved into the house in London that I'm living in now, I had a meltdown in a local tile shop (called, unfortunately, Tiles of Wisdom) about the gargantuan choice of white tiles available from which I was supposed to choose for a bathroom refurbishment. "How can you work with all these tiles?" I screamed to the shop assistant. "They all look the same." If I were French, I would not hesitate over what kind of tiles to buy in Tiles of Wisdom; I would just know.

Of course, I also know that many of the writers in this book would have a meltdown in Tiles of Wisdom. Balzac would have a tantrum about the lack of coffee provision. Maupassant would be having sex with a prostitute in the staff toilets. But this is the realization that has really made me the happiest. I do not literally mean the realization that a syphilitic French author could have sex in Tiles of Wisdom. I mean the realization that my French obsession is a bit fake and a bit sad, and it says more about me than about the French, but that it is also OK. These writers have shown me that the people I put on a pedestal have feet of clay: they are foolish and short-termist and human, just as we all are. Which is what actually makes them better role models. This, in the end, has been the thread that has pulled me close to these writers and their works: they're complicated and contradictory and ambiguous. Their lessons in happiness are the opposite of the takeaways you find in a self-help book. They don't always make sense on first reading, and they seem different every time you return to them. The characters in these books are every bit as frustrating and layered as the people we seek to form relationships with in real life.

The other thing that never quite fit into my narrative of the joy-seeking, ever-questing romantic French writers is that many of them had lives outside of their writing and to

some extent perhaps didn't even really think of themselves
as writers—and certainly not as exclusively writers. Their
creations mirrored the concerns that they fought for in other
ways: writing was a way to put their ideas across, to make their
worldview "win." And they were often doing this in a spirit of
desperation, not of passion or enthusiasm. Balzac essentially
wrote to pay debts. Victor Hugo wrote as an adjunct to his
political career, and he arguably preferred poetry to novels.
Françoise Sagan wanted to annoy her parents and make her
school friends jealous. Choderlos de Laclos hit on a happy
accident: one work that captured people's imagination at a
particular moment in time. Of course, there are "pure" writers like, perhaps, Duras or Flaubert, who could only ever have
lived as writers. But overall the lives of all these writers—and
the lives of the characters they create—demonstrate the utter
messiness and chaos of life. Hardly anyone is entirely admirable. Hardly anyone has a plan. And hardly anyone's life is
entirely worth emulating.

This runs contrary to the idea that you should try to
be more French. Because according to that rationale, you
shouldn't try to be like anyone. But now that I can see the
deception for what it is, I'm still not ready to give it up. I would
like to have it both ways. Or, as the French say, *"avoir le beurre
et l'argent du beurre."* ("To have the butter and the money for
the butter.") I can live in the truth and still wear rose-colored
vintage Yves Saint Laurent spectacles sourced on Etsy. If anything, now more than ever, I'm ready to go full-on French.
Because if the French are not that special and they're actually
just like the rest of us . . . Well, that makes it easier to become
one of them. Now that I am in my mid-forties, I have moments
of thinking, "Perhaps when I am fifty—or sixty—I will rename

myself Vivienne and force everyone to call me by that name."
I think Stendhal would approve.

As for the myth of French happiness, I'm not sure anyone really ever believed that the French are particularly happy people. In fact, in well-being surveys (don't you hate a well-being survey?), they always come out terribly. When Wrike, a Silicon Valley "work management platform," commissioned a Happiness Index of four thousand workers in the UK, US, Germany, and France, they found that the French were the most miserable in their jobs. The Americans were the happiest. This is self-evident to me. Of course the French hate their jobs: they are too busy enjoying their real lives too much. Work is not real life to them. And of course the Americans report that they are happy at work, because—unlike the French—the Anglo-Saxon model insists that our work is our identity and we must find a way to express ourselves professionally; otherwise we have failed in life. The French say, "Why bother with work when there is wine, cheese, and sex?" (Obviously the happiest French people would be those who had found a way to work in the wine, cheese, or sex industries.)

So the business of French happiness is really a matter of how you manage your circumstances. It's a state of mind accessible to all of us. It's not that French people are happy all the time or even that they are happier than we are. It's just that they have managed life in such a way that they value the pleasures of life and accept that these cannot be experienced 24/7; they need to some extent to be compartmentalized. It's also true that caring about what makes life meaningful and examining this in a serious way is woven into the French way of life. Children are taught philosophy from the age of eleven, and it is a compulsory subject until the age of eighteen, and has been a compulsory subject since 1808. In *"philo,"* as French students call it, they are called upon to write four-hour essays on such subjects as "Can a scientific truth be dangerous?" And "Is it one's own responsibility to find happiness?" When asked about the purpose of teaching philosophy to young people, the French national education inspector replied that the main objective of the course was to "develop a capacity for personal reflection." Imagine if this was part of your national life: the insistence that you reflect on yourself. This is major.

If I am going to take on any mentality, that's the one I want. But can you escape into a different mentality by learning another language? Can you inhabit a new frame of mind by having concepts (or just words) that are more, well, French? Can you think yourself happier by borrowing from another language? Without this being a conscious thought on my part when I first started learning French, it was this attitude that really motivated me from the very first moment I encountered the language. It wasn't possible for me to be somewhere else physically, because I was eleven and had to live at home with my parents. If I had tried to run away to France or any other place, I would have been brought home by the police. But to learn another language that was not my own? Well, that was safe and legal and allowed me to be somewhere else mentally without anyone having to send out a search party.

I discovered many years later that there is a whole academic debate about the effect of language on our mind-set and identity. The question "Does the language you speak affect the way you speak?" is explored in Guy Deutscher's wonderful book *Through the Language Glass: Why the World Looks Different in Different Languages*. Deutscher explores the ways in which we are all tempted to argue that the languages we know—whether they are the languages we have grown up with or the languages that we have learned to love—are special in some way. We tend to argue that languages have certain characteristics (German is practical, French is romantic, and so on). Throughout history, he explains, there has been a tendency—especially among show-offs who wanted to display how many languages they spoke, to say that certain languages are suitable for certain purposes or moods. Deutscher quotes Charles V, King of Spain, who used to say that he spoke "Spanish to God, Italian to women, French to men, and German to my horse." (I feel sorry for the women who didn't speak any Italian who had to listen to him prattling on, but possibly they were very glad not to understand a word of his pompous nonsense. I imagine the horse rolled its eyes quite a lot too.) There is certainly evidence that the language we speak affects the way we "see" the world. In Russian, for example, there are two words for blue, and they do not correspond entirely as to the difference we might make in English between "light blue" and "dark blue." Arguably Russians see these as two completely new colors.

But what evidence is there that we can feel things differently in another language? Apart from the obvious sentimental proof: my tears of joy, melting self-hate, and inebriation when I have had a few too many glasses of Sancerre and my French has suddenly become very coherent and particularly beautiful. Or it seems that way to me, anyway. Probably to anyone listening it sounds like fluent drunkese, a language we are all familiar with trying and failing to understand. What if a connection in another language can make us experience new emotions? Or experience our emotions on a deeper level? Isn't that the key to a very real and exciting kind of happiness and ultimate connection? I have definitely felt it while rereading these books.

On the other hand, one of the unfortunate and unintended consequences of the writing of this book is that I have become completely obsessed with syphilis. It seems unlikely that I need to worry about contracting it (I have been married to the same man for some twenty years and we are both very unadventurous British-type persons). But I feel a curious affinity with the many French writers I loved as an innocent teenager who turned out to be ravaged by this hideous disease. I suppose I knew at the time that I first discovered these writers that they were nineteenth-century types who loved nothing better than cavorting with prostitutes and accumulating genital sores. But, blinded by the many beautiful things they wrote, I never really put much thought into the lives they must have been living and the physical and mental pain that must have tortured them for most of their lives. I also know way more about dabbing cankers with mercury pills than I ever wanted to think about. I take no joy from that. But it does make me shrug (and say *"Bof"*) and think, "Well, nobody's perfect."

Ultimately the lesson here is not so much about happiness as about authenticity. Because unless you feel that you're being an authentic, honest, real version of yourself, there's no way you can be happy. I used to think that if I could be more authentically French, then that would make me happy. At one point, I even went to see a French speech therapist to ask if she could eliminate my accent when I spoke French. She looked at me sadly but kindly and said, "Yes, it can be done. But isn't your English accent a part of who you are?" I now realize that what we all need to be—especially as we get older—is a version of ourselves that we feel most comfortable with and that feels the most real to us. For me, that will always have elements of French fancy. But not if those elements mean erasing parts of who I really am, even if those parts are the bits of myself I like the least.

There's something very useful in the book of Françoise Sagan's recorded interviews when she talks about how she coped with "being Françoise Sagan." People wanted her to be all sorts of things that she thought she wasn't: she felt as if she was a cartoon character in a comic book. They gave her all kinds of self-contradictory labels: the perverted, scandalous young girl; the ungrateful ignoramus who had no idea how lucky she was; the fake whose book had been written by someone else—the crazy woman, quite simply. She particularly resented hearing about the "DIY Sagan kit" a journalist had written about: a bottle of whiskey, a typewriter, a bottle of pills, a collection of Karl Marx editions, an Aston Martin. "I never took pills. And I know very little about Karl Marx," she wrote. Whiskey, typewriter, and Aston Martin, sure, those she had to concede. They were indeed part of her arsenal.

In the end, Sagan decided that the best thing she could do was to use this mask to hide behind. Once she put on "the mask of the legend," she could actually be herself, mixing up the myth (which she admitted had elements of truth) and her real self. She gave up trying to prove that she wasn't who the press said she was ("the woman who is rolling around with her millions, mowing old ladies down in the street with her Jaguar and who lives to shock"). As for the money, she was never sure whether people resented more the fact that she earned it or the fact that she spent it. The mask, clearly, was a comfort, as she could be what she wanted to be: a mix of both herself and the person others expected her to be.

I recently found another archive clip of Françoise Sagan and her magnificent, death-defying driving. In it, Sagan is driving a small but stubborn car through the streets of Paris at great speed. (It's not the same as the car she was driving in the Clive James documentary. I'm guessing she crashed that one.) Her messy blond hair is flying in the wind and she is smoking a cigarette, gesticulating wildly, talking even faster than she is driving. This time we don't see the interviewer who is sitting next to her, but we imagine them to be terrified out of their wits. As she talks away, she juggles the cigarette, occasionally bothering to maneuver the steering wheel haphazardly, as if it were some kind of random afterthought that doesn't have that much to do with the driver. The car approaches a giant mess of traffic at the Arc de Triomphe and looks almost certain to crash. Swearing, beeping her horn, and gesturing about the idiocy of other drivers, Sagan puts her foot on the accelerator and spins her way around the world's most famous glorified *rond-point*, almost daring other cars to get in her way. This is Frenchness at its height: enthusiastic, devil-may-care, selfish, reckless, glorious, glamorous, messy. You could describe Sagan as many things, many of them terrible. But, God, did she know how to live. Sure, it's dangerous. But you still want a piece of it. There are worse ways to say goodbye to sadness.

ACKNOWLEDGMENTS

Many of us have been heavily influenced by books we read at a certain time in our lives, especially the literature we discover as "classics" in late adolescence. Several key people understood this and helped this book to come to light, not just because they "got" the idea but because of their passion as readers. *Au Revoir, Tristesse* would not have been written without the encouragement, understanding, and exacting precision of my most excellent editor, Jamison Stoltz, a man who is the definition of "smart" in both British and American English. He managed to exorcise most of my extreme tendencies toward British turns of phrase. Any that remain are exclusively my fault. A big thank-you also to copy editor Jean Hartig for such careful and empathetic work. I am grateful—always—to my agent, Cathryn Summerhayes, who is always on the side of both the writer and the reader.

I first started learning French at the age of eleven and am very grateful to my first French teacher, Mrs. Langdon, whose enthusiasm and exuberance definitely had a hand in my early interest. My long-term French teacher at school, the late Mr. Harley, had a huge impact on my life. His passion for language and literature was infectious, and he always brought a sense of humor into things. I studied French at university because of him and followed in his footsteps by attending Selwyn College, University of Cambridge.

At Selwyn, my inspiring and beady-eyed tutor was Dr. Michael Tilby, a patient and generous teacher of French literature. He gifted me with a lifelong obsession of "exploring the ambiguity," a habit that never gets old and can be fruitfully applied to most things in life. Possibly I drank too much of his sherry (and other things) on occasion, and for that I apologize. At university my French language teacher was Jean-Pierre Daraux, whose inability to suffer fools gladly or tolerate the smallest mispronunciation left all his students with far better language skills than we deserved. While I was a student, I did my work experience at *Ouest-France* newspaper in Saint-Lô, and I will always remember the kindness shown to me there by Alain Thomas and Isabelle Lê.

I have been lucky to have had the support of many close friends who tolerated my moaning and procrastination during the writing and editing process of this book. They know who they are. A special shout-out to Fiona and Liam Grundy, who were kind enough to find me a place where I could write in peace. Thanks as always to my family and especially to my sister, Trudy, who teaches French day in, day out without (hardly ever) complaining.

A NOTE ON OTHER WRITERS

The works examined here were chosen because they represented my own introduction to French literature. Life before
the twenty-first century being what it was, the writers who have
ended up in this collection are all white and mostly men. Clearly
this isn't an ideal state of affairs. Although I don't really like the
expression "pale, male, and stale," as no one can help being pale
or male, and staleness is a matter of individual judgement, all
the same, if any group of people is at least two of these things,
then it's the authors of the French classics. I like to think that
none of these authors is stale, however. Otherwise I would not
have included them in this collection. But while their works may
be evergreen and unpredictable, their places in identity politics
are very predictable.

There's no easy solution to remedying this kind of cultural
dominance. The classics of the past four centuries were, by definition and of necessity, skewed toward the works of white men
because that was the social category that contained the individuals
who were most likely to be able to find the time and the financial
capacity to write. And as a consequence they were the most likely to
be published. When I was at university in the mid-1990s, certainly
feminism and postcolonialism were discussed, and we were encouraged to read Simone de Beauvoir, Hélène Cixous, and Marguerite
Duras. But there was no extreme questioning of the curriculum in
the way that there is—quite rightly—now.

I didn't want to perform some act of extreme revisionism by
including writers not traditionally classed as "classic French authors"
in this collection, as there's something wrong about insisting that
someone most people have never heard of is on a par with Proust.
Sure, there are many writers who might have occupied a different
place in the narrative if things were different. But, the fact is, things

weren't different. And we can't rewrite history or change the esteem in which these writers were held in their lifetime.

I'm conscious, though, that there are so many other writers worth discovering and deserving mention. For a shortcut to finding recent and contemporary female authors and writers of color, it's worth looking up the Prix Femina. This is a prize created in 1904. Interestingly, the point of this prize is that it has an all-female jury, but it rewards work in the French language by both men and women. I have discovered many authors through this prize, including Marguerite Yourcenar, Marie NDiaye (the first black woman to win the Prix Goncourt, the other important French literary prize), Chantal Thomas, Gwenaëlle Aubry, Nancy Huston, Dai Sijie, and François Cheng.

As with all these examples, I'm biased toward the names I know and have read. In recent years I have discovered Irène Némirovsky, Nathalie Sarraute, Maryse Condé, Leïla Slimani, Annie Ernaux, Fatou Diome, Véronique Tadjo, and Rashid Boudjedra. Two of my personal long-standing favorites are Marie Darrieussecq and Amélie Nothomb. Darrieussecq is one of France's most prolific and exciting contemporary novelists. Her nonfiction book on motherhood, *Le Bébé*, is funny, profound, and philosophical. The novel that made her name, *Pig Tales: A Novel of Lust and Transformation*, was translated into thirty languages. Called *Truismes* in the original French, it's about a woman who starts turning into a pig. Nothomb is a Belgian writer who writes in French. Her father was a diplomat, and she lived all over the world as a child. Her best-known work in translation is *Fear and Trembling*, a wonderfully funny and clever novella about a Western woman faced with the tricky realities of life while working in a Japanese corporation in Tokyo.

I'm just scratching the surface here in terms of writers who may be regarded in the future in the way that we regard Proust now. If you have more suggestions to share with others, please let me know @vivgroskop on social media or at my website, www.vivgroskop.com.

RECOMMENDED READING

As you will have worked out from my account of my obsessive French-learning in my late teens and the horrific University of Cambridge reading list, I have been reading around these authors for more than thirty years. So this list is not a bibliography. Instead I wanted to compile an accessible list of books I really recommend that are suitable for people who are not quite as obsessive. In writing *Au Revoir, Tristesse*, I tried to lean on specific translations and biographies that would be easy for readers to find as a follow-up after finishing this book. I've worked from a series of translated texts. In many cases I've lost track over the years of which translation I read when and how many times I've dipped into the original. In any case, I'm not a snob about translation, and the ones I've suggested here were closest to hand. They're not a suggestion of "the best translation," as I don't believe in such things.

Bonjour Tristesse by Françoise Sagan
There's a wonderful Penguin Modern Classics edition from 2013 translated by Heather Lloyd with a foreword by Rachel Cusk. Don't be surprised when the book (novella, really) suddenly finishes—because, as I've mentioned, it is disarmingly short—and you get a bonus story (also a novella), "A Certain Smile." If you can read in French, I recommend *Sagan à Toute Allure* by Marie-Dominique Lelièvre (Folio, 2009) and *Je Ne Renie Rien* by Françoise Sagan (Livre de Poche, 2015).

À La Recherche du Temps Perdu by Marcel Proust
I mostly tackled Proust in French when I was at university. But I have since read translations by C. K. Scott Moncrieff and Christopher Prendergast. For an excellent read on Proust's life, I recommend Edmund White's *Marcel Proust: A Life* (Penguin Modern Biographies, 2009). For background on

the American fascination with France and French writers that informed some of my ideas about Proust and other writers here, I recommend *Why France? American Historians Reflect on an Enduring Fascination* by Laura Lee Downs and Stephane Gerson (Cornell University Press, 2009). I also need to give a nod to Alain de Botton's *How Proust Can Change Your Life* (Picador, 2006), which encouraged me to give Proust another go after my slightly miserable student reading experience of him.

Gigi by Colette
There are many translations of *Gigi*, but I worked from one of the most recent ones by Roger Senhouse for Vintage Classics, *Gigi* and *The Cat* (2001). Judith Thurman's *Secret of the Flesh: A Life of Colette* (Ballantine, 2000) is a fantastic read. For French readers, *Mathilde de Morny: La Scandaleuse Marquise et Son Temps* by Claude Francis (Perrin, 2000) is informative and entertaining.

Les Misérables by Victor Hugo
Norman Denny's 1982 translation for Penguin Classics more than stands the test of time. And Graham Robb's biography *Victor Hugo* (W.W. Norton, 1998) is full of all the color and storytelling you would expect from Robb. (See also *La Cousine Bette* by Honoré de Balzac.)

Les Liaisons Dangereuses by Choderlos de Laclos
See Helen Constantine's 2007 translation for Penguin Classics. As I've said, of all the books here (apart from perhaps *Bonjour Tristesse*), this is the one I really recommend reading in French if you are learning the language. I have the Folio (Gallimard) 2006 edition.

L'Amant by Marguerite Duras
I worked from Barbara Bray's 2012 translation for Harper Perennial Modern Classics. Highly recommended: Laure

Adler's *Marguerite Duras: A Life* (University of Chicago, 2001). Just a fantastic biography.

Madame Bovary by Gustave Flaubert
I went old-school for this translation and found the edition I first had at university: Alan Russell's translation for Penguin Classics: *Madame Bovary: A Story of Provincial Life*. For biography, Geoffrey Wall's *Flaubert: A Life* (Farrar, Straus and Giroux, 2002). See also *Flaubert's Parrot* by Julian Barnes (Vintage, 2009).

Cyrano de Bergerac by Edmond Rostand
I used Carol Clark's 2006 translation for Penguin Classics. In French I really enjoyed trying to read *L'Autre Monde* (*Les États et Empires de la Lune; Les États et Empires du Soleil*) by Cyrano de Bergerac (Folio, 2004) in order to get a measure of Cyrano himself as a writer. It's an incredibly dense and eccentric piece of early science fiction. Robert Darnton's *The Great Cat Massacre and Other Episodes in French Cultural History* (Basic Books, 2009) is a wonderful book and gave me so much to think about in regard to the world that lots of these writers were writing in.

Bel-Ami by Guy de Maupassant
The 1975 translation by Douglas Parmée for Penguin Classics is recognized as superb. (I know I said I don't approve of rating translations, but I just thought I'd mention that.) Sorry to say, but there's not much point in trying to understand many French writers of a certain period without reading Deborah Hayden's *Pox: Genius, Madness, and the Mysteries of Syphilis* (Basic Books, 2003). You're welcome!

Le Rouge et Le Noir by Stendhal
Roger Gard's 2002 translation for Penguin Classics is so fluid and easy to read. For background, one of the best biographical resources is Francesco Manzini's *Stendhal: Critical Lives* (Reaktion Books, 2019).

La Cousine Bette by Honoré de Balzac
Marion Crawford's 2004 translation for Penguin Modern
Classics is not the one I would have had at university, but
reading it felt like settling into an easy chair. *Balzac: A Biography*
by Graham Robb (W.W. Norton) is the ultimate in brilliant
biographical writing.

L'Étranger by Albert Camus
See Sandra Smith's 2013 translation, *The Outsider*, for Penguin
Modern Classics. For further reading, it's worth looking at
Kamel Daoud's *The Meursault Investigation* (Other Press), a
postcolonialist fictional response to *L'Étranger*. Alice Kaplan's
nonfiction account *Looking for* The Stranger: *Albert Camus
and the Life of a Literary Classic* (University of Chicago, 2016)
is great.